Freedom in Your Relationship with Food

Freedom in Your Relationship with Food

An Everyday Guide

Myra E. Lewin

ISBN-13: 9780692953907
ISBN-10: 0692953906

Table of Contents

Acknowledgements

The sweet support of wonderful students, clients and friends inspires my journey through life. The publication of this book would not have been possible without those who were open to guidance from this information. The individuals who provided their encouragement and love to the process of this book include Shannon Wianecki, Vanessa Massey, Brenda Newton, Dana Stoltz Gray, Alfredo Fernandez-Bussy, and many others; to all of you I express my deepest appreciation and gratitude.

Each day I consider the wonder of life. I offer appreciation and love to the great teachers and mystics who patiently passed on the wisdom and teachings of Yoga and Ayurveda to all of us. Through these teachings, I connect to my Divine source and all that is.

May you see who you truly are as eternal spirit. Remember it each day and in each moment. Peace to all.

Introduction

I invite you to embark on a journey into the truth of your personal relationship with food and eating. Having picked up this book, you have already begun. It is time to take stock of your beliefs and behaviors concerning this essential aspect of human experience. Wake up from mainstream habits and unconscious attitudes. A "magic pill" that removes the need to make responsible choices does not exist. This book is a guide to raising your consciousness toward food and eating using Ayurvedic principles. Yoga practitioners of all levels will find it particularly inviting.

Though these pages provide a path to freedom, you will need to do the traveling. The adventure ahead holds what, at first, may seem formidable challenges. Sages say that the only way out is through, and I assure you that willingness and an open mind are all you need. Aspects of your life beyond diet will benefit from the self-knowledge and inner strength that you can discover here. Calling to you from the other side are those of us who have found a gentle harmony with eating that imbues daily living with vitality and ease.

Although the information in this book is straightforward, staying focused and present while reading may sometimes be difficult. Reading about changing patterns related to food and eating often arouses layers of programming from deep in the subconscious and unconscious layers of your being. It may trigger desires to act compulsively. I encourage you to turn away and not give in to these unconscious desires. Be persistent in keeping a positive, focused mindset as you read. This may require rereading the same paragraph many times in order to absorb the information. As the programming and unconscious attitudes start to leave you, it may feel like a battle or an uncomfortable delay. In this book, you will find simple ways to validate your innermost truth and move beyond the discomfort from change.

The first part of this book will deepen your understanding of your relationship with food. It addresses how that relationship reflects in all of your interactions and explores new possibilities. The next sections provide simple, natural approaches to meeting your true needs in terms of eating and relating with others. Finally, there are reference guides, a list of ailments and suggested solutions, and simple practices for you to work with.

A great teacher once said to me "Don't believe a word I say. Work with what I have to offer and learn from your own experience." I suggest the same to you. Beliefs can be limiting, but your experience has infinite possibilities.

Finding Your Truth

OUR RELATIONSHIP WITH FOOD

A re you concerned about what and how you eat? What are the factors you consider when making decisions about food and eating? Perhaps your main concerns are cost, convenience, flavor, traditions, nourishment, pleasure, weight control, or health. Does the information from the media confuse you? What is the role of food in your life? Are you at peace with your relationship to food and eating? Many people ask these questions because the answers are not clear and sometimes difficult to face. I suggest take the time now to answer these questions for yourself and this book will be of maximum use to you.

An old story says that if a frog jumps into a cooking pot, it realizes that the water is fatally hot and jumps back out immediately. However, if the frog gets into a cool pot and it heats up gradually, he will not jump out. The frog will adapt to the gradually heating water to the point of killing itself without realizing what is happening. This is a good metaphor for what is happening in modern culture with consumption and particularly with the consumption of food and drink.

Modern culture has lost touch with the sacred nature of food and eating. Some would say this began when agrarian living replaced nomadic living—when manipulating nature replaced flowing with nature. Others say it began when organized religion established rules about what to eat and when. Some would contend the change came when industrialization shifted work away from home and nature and into a factory. Still others would blame the invention of radio, television, computers, and other electronics, which have separated us further from nature, each other, and ourselves.

In the second half of the twentieth century, science and technology became the answers for everything. Food was most highly regarded if it came out of a fabricated container. It was "convenient" if no preparation was required. If someone else prepared it in an unseen restaurant kitchen, it was deemed "gourmet." Both of these approaches held high social regard and reflected a person's wealth.

Now, in this time of so-called scientific progress, many foods are genetically engineered and come from an environment polluted with pesticides, herbicides, and chemical fertilizers. Your food likely traveled hundreds if not thousands of miles to get to you. As it ages, all food loses flavor, prana (life force), nutritional content, and benefit to you as a consumer. Eating lifeless food made appealing with ingredients such as salt and sugar dulls your taste buds and knocks your system out of balance. You then look for more food with stronger added tastes to satisfy your senses—a vicious cycle.

Are you eating in haste, in the car, at your desk, or standing in the kitchen? Are you eating with distractions such as radio, books, television, phone or computers? If you are, you are eating and drinking with little to no consciousness. The price for unconscious eating is enormous. It includes disturbed digestion, obesity, suffering, and disease. According to numerous scientific studies from around the world, diet is a significant factor in the three leading causes of death which include heart disease, cancer, stroke and diabetes.[1]

The external demands, numerous distractions, and fast pace of modern life may lead you to forget your priorities. Disconnection from your authentic self is the norm in this environment. Saying yes to things that are not in your best interest is easy. Families no longer eat together regularly. These days, eating food prepared by someone you do not know is common. Perhaps each of these changes has contributed something to the gap between daily consumption choices and your sense of self.

I recently had a student say to me, "I don't think I even have a relationship with food. I think I inherited my parents' relationships with food and have never thought about it." Many people have a similar response when queried about their relationship with food.

When eating and self-care become habitual and unconscious, the result is feelings of emptiness and disconnection. This approach to living may seem convenient and easy, but it encourages an unconscious attitude toward all of life. The media advertises new fixes that promise to make everything feel okay. However, "everything" stays the same. Many people skim through life from one new approach to the next. Then they wonder why they feel anxious, bored, and discontented.

Some people are very aware that improvement in their eating habits leads to feeling better. However, maintaining the connection between how you feel and what you eat is difficult for many. When stress or special occasions come up, reverting to unconscious eating habits from childhood, cultural practices, or advertising is easy. The slip backward isn't noticed until the consequences, such as indigestion, sluggishness, or weight gain, cause significant discomfort.

Often the excuse for slipping back into poor habits is self-justified with ideas like "It is my reward for being good" or "I work so hard, I deserve a treat." This attitude develops in childhood. When children are encouraged to feed their feelings instead of experiencing them, they learn to look at food as mood altering and a reward. Compulsion and obesity are a natural result.

In the twentieth century, the power of individuals' connection to food, nature, and each other diminished. The government and the media claimed to possess all of the answers. Mechanical guidelines for food and eating became a part of school health classes for children. Previously this information had been a natural part of growing up, passed on within the family home. Then, the government and food companies established recommended food groups and intake, and the public followed. Our lack of self-trust and our blind faith in authority begins with school-age programming. Today, we are trained to follow official recommendations while disregarding personal experience and intuition. No wonder it all seems confusing and mysterious.

The media and other sources bombard us with superficial cures for our woes. Buy one more thing and you will feel better. Change your hair color one more time and all will be well. Eat or drink this super food and you will feel fantastic all of the time.

While the primary focus in this book is on the food and beverages you put in your mouth, the same principles apply in all types of consumption. Food is potentially anything you consume through your senses, including the mouth, nose, eyes, ears, and skin. This includes:

- Substances you put in your mouth,
- Supplements and vitamins,
- Drugs of all types (prescription or otherwise),
- Beverages,
- What you watch (television, movies, computer, video games, etc.),
- Sounds you listen to (music, background noise, conversation, etc.),
- Atmospheres you breathe and take in through all sense organs (even what you cannot see),
- Products you choose to put on your body (skin, hair, scalp, nails, etc.).

Unconscious consumption in any of these areas leads to disconnection and unhappiness. How many of these items do you consume based on propaganda or advertising? Allowing companies whose first motive is profit to play the primary role in how you nourish yourself and your family diminishes self-confidence. The result is confusion and the inability to be clear about what is inherently right for you.

Do not naively hand over your decision-making power to someone else. I hear people repeatedly say "I don't trust myself" and "I have no discipline" in relation to food. This disconnection breeds an increasing occurrence of obesity, addiction, and disease in both adults and children.

Knowing and understanding where your food comes from is another common area of unconsciousness. Many people have no idea how or where their food is grown or how the animal was fed and treated. They assume that if there is a problem, something or someone else will handle it. Operating with the idea that someone else is taking care of your food supply is an unconscious approach that has led to serious health problems in modern culture.

The government attempts to regulate the safe production and distribution of food. The difficulties of overseeing such an enormous task and fear-driven overreaction often result in policies not in the best interest of your individual health. For example, when one apple juice producer has a problem, the requirements for all apple juice production change based on the fear of another problem. The additional processing degrades the quality of the juice provided to you, the consumer.

Consumers rely on packaging to tell them where the food comes from and how it is processed and handled. Again, this is helpful information but often not the whole story. Packaging contains unidentified chemicals, and many items are not required to be included in the ingredients list. Having all of the information might significantly affect your purchasing decisions. Ignoring the true meaning of food for you, including the why, what, and how you eat, increases disconnection. This cultivates uncertainty and a sense of emptiness.

"Freedom is being able to eat whatever I want, when I want it." Many people live by this lie. Using food to strive for a sense of power leads to compulsion and addiction. Perhaps this started when mom was deciding how and what you would eat and you rebelled. Sometimes rebellion about food relates to feelings not related to food. Mother is the first main connection in this life and to the sacred. If this connection is disturbed, there can be disturbance in our relationship to food and nature.

Your upbringing combined with your heritage, cultural programming, schooling, and media all deeply affect your behavior around food and eating. Realize that you cannot develop a personal relationship with food until you overcome the current unconscious patterns.

Many people create a false sense of relationship and connection to others through eating, movies, social gatherings, and fantasy thinking. You may find that when you relate to others you are actually trying to get something, such as relief from loneliness or the feeling of emptiness. From this, an illusion of connection develops. In reality, you are demanding, "I want you to be what I need" or "I want you to fit into my picture of what I want." This type of relating can work for a short time. Then reality leaks in and difficulties arise. The relationship is actually about getting something rather than learning about and accepting the other person and yourself. The results are depression, disharmony, and imbalance on all levels: physically, mentally, psychically, and spiritually. This principle also applies to your relationship to food. When you eat, are you demanding comfort, entertainment, or the fulfillment of some other need?

Addressing your relationship to food and consumption goes straight to your core beliefs. For example, you might think that cooking is too much trouble, or dislike doing it. These beliefs often reflect a lack of self-worth or the desire for someone else to meet your needs. They lead to unresolved feelings that will direct your life until you turn inward and release them. Recognizing the lies in those beliefs will allow you to change them.

A conscious relationship with food is an essential part of living in balance. This book will help you find the source of your actions, identify underlying problems, and eliminate them. By doing so and learning to curb your desires gently in all areas of life, you will strengthen your mind and allow the opportunity to make choices in support of your well-being. This may require a change of attitude. It will likely require changing some products and foods you use. Realize there are many alternatives to the typical commercial products available. Many of them are less expensive and very simple.

IMPROVING THE RELATIONSHIP

My own experience of thirty years traveling along the path from confusion to clarity, disease to health, and disconnection to union led me to write this book. The information contained here comes both from my personal experience and from insights gained in extensive work with students and clients.

When I began this journey, I was significantly out of balance and had been so most of my life. I thought I was doomed to a life of "digestive problems and feeling slightly crazy." Switching to healthier food and eliminating meat was a first step for me, but it did not solve most of the challenges I faced with health and weight control.

Many years later, I was studying Yoga in India when an introduction to Ayurveda convinced me to open my mind further. Only when I learned of feeling well and balanced from the Ayurvedic perspective did I realize the possibilities beyond what I had known. Discovering how to eat in a balanced way, in concert with my nature along with strengthening my digestion opened up a new way of being in life.

I found that clearing out old information and learning how to sift through new information dissolved the complexity, and the process became easier.

Some people hope to change how they feel by adding spiritual practices to their life. Although spiritual practices help, they will not remove the depression, anxiety, and discontent as long as the same unconscious attitudes remain. To spiritualize life means to practice consciousness in all areas of life, each day. This book provides simple, natural approaches to meeting your true needs in terms of food, eating, and your relationships with others and the earth. This is not a black-and-white topic but is rather many shades of gray. This dance of life is a work of art where science is a tool.

Integrating simple tools and practices into your life will help you increase your awareness. Awareness is relaxed and expansive. With your new awareness, there will be no place for craving and addiction to grow. As you utilize this new awareness, you awaken your consciousness and connection to the Divine source. This awakening will lead you to make healthier choices, feel stronger and more peaceful. Your perspective will change. You will learn to trust yourself and your ability to find your truth. You will find acceptance and patience with others.

Nurturing your connection to food and eating will bring great healing for you, your family, and your community. It will open your connection to nature. As you grow and become more conscious and peaceful, connection to the sacred will come into your eating and daily life. Right now, this may seem far away or unattainable, but I assure you it is possible.

Be true to yourself, be an explorer. Let life be an adventure, day by day.

The suggestions made throughout this book are just that. Use the book as a practical source of information to work with one piece at a time. You will be asked to notice what is real for you rather than what "should be" or what "a study says." Take time to answer the questions and write out the lists recommended in each chapter. I think you will find the suggestions are simple, yet sometimes challenging.

I am recommending a path other than the mainstream. Flowing with the strongest current leads to mechanical living and little to no joy in life. Stop imposing conditions on your life; surrender to the Divine rhythm. It requires courage to do what is right for you regardless of what others are doing. It requires courage to turn away from societal norms and to be responsible for your own health and well-being. This kind of strength is your birthright. If you are willing, these pages can help you.

LETTING GO OF THE ILLUSION OF CONTROL

For you, control might mean organizing, being in charge, or having power over something. These definitions apply to taking care of your bills, your health, and aspects of your work. However, when your actions become a performance to please others rather than an expression of your own truth, this is not true control. It is an illusion.

Another illusion of control is thinking you can control one aspect of your life by controlling another. For instance, perhaps you equate controlling your weight with controlling your health. The control over your health is an illusion because your food choices may accommodate your weight, but not necessarily your health.

The fear of losing control will ultimately deplete your energy and well-being. Unless you learn to give up your illusions of control and develop a harmonious relationship with food, poor health and unhappiness will grow.

When life asks you to face reality, coping mechanisms kick in to maintain your illusion and avoid the feelings. Do you experience large peaks of feeling better and valleys of feeling worse than before? In order to try to control the peaks and valleys, a drive for perfection develops. The drive for perfection can distort your sense of self and the world. This distortion makes facing reality difficult, and these extreme cycles lead to compromised vitality and ultimately more fear. Here are some examples of behaviors driven by an illusion of control:

- "Yo-yo dieting," cycles of depriving and binging.
- Fasting or cleansing followed by a binge.
- Taking large amounts of vitamins and supplements to feel high energy and be healthy.
- Emphasizing protein and low carbohydrates in meals to stay skinny.
- Eating excessive protein to build more muscle, to burn more fat, to stay thin.
- Eating and drinking only diet foods in order to deserve sugary treats.
- Eating only small portions or salads in public to show how you are watching your weight.
- Skipping breakfast in order to eat less in a day.
- Buying gym memberships or Yoga classes and not using them, but feeling like you did good to make the purchase.

- Sucking in your tummy in public to look thinner.
- Exercising excessively to make up for binging and fear of fat.
- Buying healthy food and letting it go bad in the refrigerator, but feeling good that you made the right purchase.

Think about the results you experience from each of the listed activities. If you find yourself justifying the activities, look a little closer. Be willing to make the connection between your actions and your results.

This illusion of control leads to a lack of conscious participation, which aggravates the problem. Conscious participation in your relationship to food and eating requires waking up to the reality of what is happening. It requires giving attention to the inherent needs of your body. Each of the examples above contains an unconscious delusion that contributes to low energy and poor health.

Sometimes low energy is a result of overexertion. Expecting to go continuously without proper rest, recreation, enough sleep, or vital food is unrealistic and out of balance. This drive to be "on the go" all of the time is propelled by fear and unresolved feelings related to self-worth. The myth "My value is based on how much I do" is running your life. You are in the doing, and not being in life.

Obsession over food and eating may be your primary choice for dealing with feelings. If the obsession stays in your head as a dark secret, fears grow. Fear of the unknown builds when you are feeling disconnected. This fear will fuel obsessive-compulsive behavior. Even when treated therapeutically, real and lasting change from obsessive-compulsive eating is unlikely without restoring some connection to your true sense of self.

The ego, or self-centered conscience, attaches itself to the illusion of being in control. An acronym for ego is Edging God Out, referring to the use of excessive self-centered will. The ego in its perfectionism wants to be right at any price, regardless of whether or not you accomplish your goal. The ego is just as happy to say, "See, I was right, I'm no good because I couldn't stick with it." This type of thinking keeps you from your truth. It keeps you from the peaceful, joy-filled life that is available to you.

Swami Paramahamsa Yogananda, a great Yogi in the early twentieth century, compared the ego to an invincible warrior no one can defeat. He said the only way to defeat the ego is to surrender. While writing this book, I sometimes became fearful and would say to myself, "Who wants to hear what I have to say anyway?" In reality, this was the ego wanting to make everything just about me. I realized I could stay stuck in fear and never finish this book. Or, I could walk through the fear and grow as a human being. A very wise person suggested that I simply put forth my best effort and surrender the results. Surrendering leads to humility in life. Humility is having a right-sized view of yourself: not too little and not too big. When you are humble, life is friendlier and more fruitful.

Surrender requires self-honesty. Honesty with yourself is difficult when caught in the cyclical insanity of compulsive eating and consumption. When you become willing to be honest about what is happening, there are approaches available to help you break the cycle. As you deal with the feelings that are driving the addiction, you must develop a spiritual foundation to support your reconnection to your innermost self. This is critical for lasting change.

Once you have surrendered and recognize that you are caught in a destructive cycle, you must acknowledge and face the problem (eating compulsively, for example) fueling the cycle. The possibility for real change exists only when you are ready to give up the addictive thinking and behavior. This requires letting go of the story line you associate with this identity and accepting reality. Without accepting reality, life becomes like a game of ping-pong—bouncing back and forth between old habits and trying new approaches. Mental, physical, and spiritual health difficulties result.

Once you perceive and accept reality, focus on rooting out the underlying feelings that drive the old behavior. These feelings usually involve anger and fear. The ego identifies with and attaches to these feelings. It hides behind them for the illusion of protection. For example, you might use anger and resistance toward your mother to protect you from becoming like her, all the while becoming more and more like her. Another example is letting fear of someone seeing you overeat dictate your eating patterns. A third example is staying angry with a previous partner to prevent being hurt again. The notion that harboring these feelings protects you from the pain in your life is a lie.

Each feeling inside of you, you have already experienced. You can continue to carry them around, or not. Choose to shine the light of your consciousness on them. Allow yourself to feel the feelings and experience them fully. Some part of you might feel like you could die from the experience or that the feelings will never stop. You will not die from experiencing feelings. Holding on to the destructive feelings will bring you suffering. Let go, and it will be finished. Allow the feeling(s) to pass. The identity you exude includes the accumulation of your unresolved feelings, but these feelings and this identity are not who you truly are.

When you want to change something, first acknowledge and accept its existence. Then, make a decision inside to let it go. You can transform your shortcomings by shifting your focus. Focus your attention, and therefore your energy, on the replacement or solution. Use your enthusiastic energy to implement your new vision.

For this approach to be successful, you will need to develop and learn to rely on your connection with your innermost self. The practice of focusing on a healthy replacement will assist in clearing the path to your peaceful nature. Your sense of self will continue to grow as you clear out old beliefs and practice new ways of being.

As you select and utilize tools from this book, remember that real, long lasting change is possible. How much will you suffer before you acknowledge the need for change and then take action? My experience is that it takes whatever is necessary for each individual.

Give up the old; make space for the new. The new you without the old feelings, beliefs, and corresponding behaviors may be unfamiliar and uncomfortable. Your courage will lead you to a new sense of freedom and vitality. The following Sanskrit mantra beautifully describes this direction:

Lead us from untruth to truth
Lead us from darkness to light
Lead us from death to immortality
Om Peace, Peace, Peace
(Sanskrit Mantra from the Vedas)

YOGA AND AYURVEDA AS YOUR ANSWER

Relating freely and easily to food requires a connection to your higher self. A connection is possible when the mind quiets enough to hear your inner voice. The practices of Yoga and Ayurveda provide the tools to reestablish this connection.

Yoga is an ancient tradition consisting of practices that support connection with the source within you and within everything. There are many branches of Yoga. Each branch describes the source in its own way: the Lord of Love, Ishvara, the sun, various deities, Mother Earth, God, and nature, among others. Regardless of the branch chosen, Yoga is a grounded basis for living. It has become popular for many people to treat Yoga as a method of exercise. The physical part of Yoga can be beneficial when practiced in a balanced manner, but it is only a small part of the total tradition.

Yoga practices are a means to transform your life. They assist you to awakening and directing your consciousness using your mind. Right attitude, or how you behave in the world, is a basic premise of Yoga. Nonviolence, as in kindness, consideration and respect toward yourself and others is the foundation of right attitude. How you treat yourself in terms of internal and external cleanliness is the second premise of Yoga. The physical postures, breathing practices, and work toward mastery of the five senses will balance and expand the prana, or life force in your body. These practices clear impurities from the body, nervous system, and mind, opening the path for meditation. Over time, meditation practice can deepen, moving from an external to an internal activity. The result is greater focus, strength of mind, connection to your source, and peaceful living.

The state of Yoga is the state of union of your body, mind, and spirit. This state is a direct perception of universal truth. This union allows you to awaken to each action in your life in every moment. It allows you to find your enthusiasm and interest in life. By practicing wholeheartedly, you will come to know your innermost self. You will learn to live from that place each day. Boredom will vanish, as all of life becomes an adventure and an exploration.

You can accomplish this type of change through conscious living and practice. You can awaken your consciousness and your connection to your Divine source within.

Ayurveda is a natural companion to the Yoga tradition. The name Ayurveda translates as "the science of life or living." This five-thousand-year-old tradition addresses quality of life and longevity. Living in harmony with nature as body, mind, and spirit is integral to the practice of Ayurveda. It is not just a feel-good strategy; Ayurveda returns you to your oneness with the universe and the Divine within you. Ayurveda looks at the individual and addresses lifestyle and conscious living in unity with all of nature. It contains a beautiful basis for reconnecting to your true self through food and consumption. The focus is on restoring balance within the body, mind, and spirit. The approach is to eliminate symptoms by eliminating the cause.

Yoga and Ayurveda are both traditions with vast bodies of information and guidance. They encourage you to evolve in natural concert with your source and all that is sacred in life. Incorporating a holistic approach to these traditions as a foundation for living allows life to expand and move beyond the limitations of the mind and external circumstances.

Utilizing Ayurveda along with Yoga as a complete foundation for living became a reality for me when I started menopause in my early forties. The changes going on inside of me created emotional upheaval and confusion. I did not expect to feel so different. Although my studies suggested it was a beautiful time of change, everything I heard around me suggested misery. I was not prepared to move through this transition.

I first tried to fix the uncomfortable symptoms and make things as they were before. It did not work. I turned to Yoga and Ayurveda for support. With loving guidance from an Ayurvedic practitioner and my Yoga teacher, I realized that menopause was a natural and revealing process of being a woman.

The problem was not menopause; my out-of-balance condition and disconnection from self is what made the transition so difficult. The suggestion was to embrace the change rather than resist it. As I let go of the internal resistance, life unfolded more easily. There were times when I did not recognize myself in my body. Over eight years of menopause, I learned to be more flexible on all levels. I learned to allow myself to receive love and support in new ways and to feel good about being a mature woman.

I incorporated simple basic practices to reach a state of balance. By keeping my digestion strong and healthy, I remained healthy when others got colds and the flu. I learned to look at my tongue each morning to see the condition of my digestion. This helped me establish a conscious connection between what I put in me and what happens in my body. I learned to tell when my digestion was weak so that I could take special care to avoid problems. I learned to be aware in new ways when the body and mind needed rest. It all seemed silly to me at first, but I found that it worked. As a result of this awareness, I have more time for living and less energy spent on problems with the body and mind.

The balance and rejuvenation I experienced with appropriate Yoga practices, Ayurvedic herbs, and other supportive practices resulted in a peaceful transition. I experience more energy and freedom as a post-menopausal woman. I have more strength, flexibility, and comfort in my body than ever before. I learned to surf and enjoy it as a regular part of my life when I thought I could never get beyond an old neck injury. New opportunities that life offers, such as writing this book, have encouraged me to grow beyond my old thinking about myself. The fears of revealing more about myself, of not doing things perfectly, and not knowing the future are no longer in charge of me.

As I continue to incorporate the multidimensional approaches of Yoga and Ayurveda into my life, my life expands exponentially in all dimensions. Much of the intellectual information that once seemed so important to me is now part of the past rather than the present. Learning to live in the connection to Divine source has helped me become spiritually responsible. The gift of Yoga and Ayurveda brings freedom in living.

Yoga and Ayurveda both support healing on all levels from the inside out and the outside in since both address the cause and not just the problem. This book is an introduction to working with these great traditions. By integrating these guidelines and tools, you can lead a balanced and harmonious life. You can make these changes now, on your own. For more information go to halepule. com for extensive information on Ayurveda and Yoga.

Identifying Your Dysfunctions

DISCONNECTION AND UNCONSCIOUSNESS

Disconnection to self, and how it plays out in daily life, is one of the most important and least acknowledged challenges of living today. Modern culture is obsessed with food and eating. The media perpetuates the idea that life is about fulfilling every desire and having a luxurious lifestyle with no discomfort. What else could there be? The "more is better" mentality, when applied to food and consumption, results in obesity, toxicity and disease. The psyche attaches to pleasure and the idea of reward through eating. This attachment disrupts assimilation and absorption of nutrients in the body, leading to imbalance. When your system is out of balance, it cannot process even the best-quality food. While the food you consume is important, how and where you eat is just as important.

Many people deny or hide from their problems with consumption. They hope the looming threat of disease will just go away. Then, some new super food, diet, or drug comes out, and they jump in for a little trial period. Sometimes they feel a brief period of relief. Then they sink back into the same digestive problems, fears of weight gain, and other disturbances they suffered before. They return to unconsciousness.

Are you allowing an unconscious attitude to direct one of your most sacred and significant activities? Eating is a sacred act that intimately connects you with nature. Your strong desire to feel better about your relationship to food and eating might also be a longing for connection to your deepest self. This paradox results in feelings of disempowerment, anger, hopelessness, and lapsing into apathy. You might realize that something is not right, but not know what to do about it. It can be confusing and frustrating.

Humans will do amazingly painful things to themselves to avoid the unknown. In my experience, life has never given me more than I could handle. I do not always know how things will work out, but the unknown provides the true adventure in life.

What food is right for you? Is it the same for everyone? Many of us do not know what to eat or how to relate to food in a natural way anymore. For example, do you find yourself straying from what works best for you in order to please someone else? Are you afraid to say no to the latest new product because your friend was so persuasive and he or she might get mad at you? You think you are pleasing them by doing it their way even though it harms you. If you asked the other person, they would likely not want you to do something that harmed you. These are common situations where you might swallow your true feelings.

When food preparation and eating seems like "too much trouble," or "there just isn't enough time for it," you are not facing your truth. You may be trying to avoid conflict, or perhaps eating makes you feel "out of control." Everything else seems more important, or there are too many things to do. Thinking this way feeds the "doing" in life rather than "being" in life.

Running from your feelings pushes you to go on to the next thing before finishing and enjoying what is right in front of you. Leaving a situation before its conclusion—either physically or mentally—breeds weakness and unconsciousness. Whether you are running from a conversation or a meal, alone or with others, you are weakening your connection to your innermost self.

Unconsciousness leads you to behaviors that are not in your best interest. These behaviors create more disconnection from self and disharmony. Analyzing and criticizing life also breeds disconnection. Being consciously present in your life in a way that you can enjoy the richness and beauty of living requires your willingness and courage. Alternately, when you make changes that cultivate conscious behavior, the mind becomes stronger. Your new strength leads to balanced living and greater connection to your innermost self.

IMPRESSIONS AND SAMSKARA

Watching television or a computer is an example of consuming through your ears and eyes. Television images, sounds, and the electromagnetic field make a significant impression on your mind, body, and psyche. Sometimes you may watch television to avoid difficulties in life or to "zone out." Doing so encourages you to become unconscious to your life. It does not actually relax the body or mind. "Zoning out" is going unconscious.

Besides breeding unconsciousness, there is another danger to watching television. Have you ever watched television or a movie and felt some part of it affecting you for a long period afterward?

I once shared a meal with three young students who grew up watching television and movies and eating mostly packaged processed foods. I noticed that they primarily saw the fresh foods we were eating in terms of jingles from advertising. We all observed that they referred to characters from movies and television as if they were actual people from their past. It was startling to see the extent of the impressions advertising and programs had made.

Your mind and body are very sensitive to outside stimuli. When your nervous system is over stimulated, it begins to shut down. Your senses become dull. When something outside of you affects you deeply, you must fully experience your feelings about it and release them. If you do not accept and experience your feelings, an impression forms in the psyche, moving into your subconscious mind. It then dictates your attitude, moods, self-image, and reactions to life. In Yoga, these unresolved impressions are called *samskara*. These impressions become deeply entrenched habits of the mind that operate independently of external stimuli. They become a "rut in the road" on the path of your life. Each time you pass down that road, you go through the rut with a bump. For example, each time you eat breakfast cereal, you might think of a packaged cereal. Or, you might remember your mother scolding you for eating too fast or rushing you to catch the bus for school and experience the resulting confusion and anger over not being able to please her. Impressions of this nature influence your behavior until you shine the light on them and heal them.

Samskara retained in your mind and body may be positive or negative in nature. They often form in relation to dramatic external stimuli, particularly challenging events such as difficulty in relationships, abuse, abandonment, or rejection. Passing through these ruts is a significant part of adulthood. In other words, you experience much of daily life through your impressions, rather than through fresh observations.

Samskara accumulate if you do not deal with them. Let them heal and it fills up the ruts. You may think the movies or events you experienced are long gone, but they persist in your body and mind. Suppressing feelings imbeds them deeper into the psyche. They reap dramatic effects on your entire life, often resulting in anxiety, depression, and suffering.

You can erase past impressions as you become aware of these "old tapes" playing in your mind. You are not your feelings. They are just movements of energy. Rather than ignoring an impression, you can choose to acknowledge it and process the underlying feelings. You cannot achieve this just by talking about your feelings. Processing feelings may include being still, acknowledging your body and breath, allowing the feelings to come and go, journaling to release the feelings, and generally allowing yourself to feel and let go of whatever comes up. It includes feeling your feelings fully, without necessarily acting on them or repressing them, and then allowing them to pass. You may also want to share your experience with a trusted friend or counselor. If you let them go without resistance or judgment, feelings will often pass quickly without event.

The ego builds an identity around suppressed impressions and feelings. You start to believe that the impressions are who you are. For example, you find yourself annoyed when someone makes a comment about chocolate cake not being good for you. As you decide to let your resistance to the comment go, the energy that was stuck moves. As the energy moves, you may feel restlessness, cold, heat, or that you are in unfamiliar territory. The result is often a sense of lightness and freedom. This new, unfamiliar place may feel uncomfortable in the body and mind. Letting go of feelings from deep impressions is not always easy to do, but very rewarding and possible with conscious, focused surrender.

Conscious attention to healing and filling in the ruts in the road will help you take a "step up" energetically toward your innermost self. Consciously choosing what and how you consume is an opportunity for transformation to more fulfilled living. This new way of living includes clarity, more energy available to you, true spontaneity, and richness in all life experiences.

Most people have some samskara about being a victim. You may feel a victim of the media, peer pressure, work, commercial food companies, chemical companies, restaurants, and holidays—just to name a few. You may be running from your own sense of vulnerability or grief you are carrying. When you hide behind a victim's point of view in life, you are covering fears. Fears are False Evidence Appearing Real; in other words, the event you fear isn't happening; it exists only in your mind. If you continue to fuel it with attention, and hence your energy, you will create whatever you fear. Remember, the ego likes to be right. You can take the steps beyond this victim's point of view. Surrender the ego, let go of the desire to be right, and fully accept this very moment and life unfolding. You will see what a miraculous being you are, capable of much more than you know.

Realize that harboring the unwillingness to do what is in your best interest is a way of remaining a victim of external circumstances. This approach to living says, "If I just keep going, I won't have to deal with what is really going on inside of me." Eventually you *will* be forced to deal with it physically, emotionally, and spiritually. Why not now? Old age does not have to mean suffering.

Health problems such as "hereditary conditions" or "environmental sensitivities" may seem insurmountable. These types of limitations can easily define the ego and your way of living. Yet, transformation and growth beyond them is possible. With an open and willing attitude, your body and mind can achieve healing, harmony, and wellness, overcoming many seeming limitations.

TRUST YOUR EXPERIENCE OVER SCIENTIFIC STUDIES AND ADVERTISING

Consuming a product just because the internet, television, magazine, book, or someone else says it is a good idea is common today. Scientific studies show up in the media saying this or that food item is good for some isolated piece of human body chemistry. Many scientific studies are conducted without regard for the holistic, integrated nature of the human being and with no consideration for an individual's unique constitution. For example, some studies say that daily consumption of wine is good for controlling blood pressure. However, this claim ignores the detrimental effects of daily wine consumption. Wine is a depressant; it taxes the liver, is primarily sugar, and is addictive. Most wine grapes are grown and produced with toxic chemicals, such as sulfites.

Giving scientific research higher regard than your own experience feeds disconnection. A study can be useful to show statistical trends. However, statistical trends are not indicative of individual needs. Even when a study considers the holistic nature of the human, it does not reflect individual experience. Giving studies more weight than your own experience leads to clouded thinking, depression, dissatisfaction, and disease.

Recently, a Stanford University professor showed how marketing certain brands to children ages three to five years affected how they perceived taste. The study asked the children to sample identical foods in brand-name wrappers and unmarked wrappers. The unmarked foods always lost the taste test—even when it was the same food. The brand marketing altered the children's perception of taste. "Successful" marketing results in children who grow up with obsessive desires for brand-name products. This obsession leads to craving and suffering. Children's psyches are impressed so deeply at an early age, they grow up learning to trust outside sources to dictate what and how they eat.

Each time you disregard your ability to attend to your needs and responses to food, you breed disconnection from self and nature. Your confidence in providing for yourself diminishes and eventually disappears. You become like the children in the study.

POOR CONSUMPTION CHOICES LEAD TO ADDICTIVE BEHAVIORS

When you are feeling disconnected from your innermost self, you are more likely to consume food and drink that is not in your best interest. You may also consume it in ways that work against your good health and well-being. The following thoughts are a result of disconnection from self, leading to poor consumption choices:

- "I should eat it because it is supposed to be good for me."
- "I've heard of it on the television or Internet so it must be good."
- "The large companies are making it, so it must be okay."
- "The person marketing the product looks good."
- "The health food store says it's a best seller."

Practicing poor consumption choices leads to compulsive, addictive behaviors. Addictions can develop on many levels to many different substances and actions. The most common include food, caffeine, soda, alcohol, cigarettes, and potentially any other substance—even water.

Poor consumption choices are a coping mechanism for attempting to hide from or feed your feelings instead of experiencing them. These choices may include eating and drinking too much, buying more than is needed or is financially prudent, participating in extreme sports, playing video games, living plugged into an iPod, gambling, excessive sexual activity, and other excessive, disconnecting behaviors.

Eating over your deepest feelings, then punishing yourself for it, then seeking relief and pleasure with compulsion and food, then punishing yourself again, leads to a cycle of abuse and addiction. Using food and drink for comfort, calming down, relief from loneliness, or reward is harmful to your health. You may experience some short successes, but not a sustainable, long-term solution that brings true joy, peace, and freedom.

CHOOSING SWEETNESS OVER SUFFERING

Compulsive behavior leads to an accumulation of metabolic toxic waste, or *ama*, in all levels of your body and being. The eventual result is low energy, sluggishness, fatigue, and eventually physical and mental disease.

The ego becomes rigid in this pattern of pleasure and punishment. *Prana*, or life force, cannot flow in you when ama is present at the cellular level. See the meditation for clearing blockages and creating wellness later in this book to assist you in enhancing cellular awareness by chipping away at the ego. A saying I heard in my training is "Heaven is egoless life, and hell is life run by the ego." The ego will assure you, "It's no problem" or "You can handle it." Meanwhile, you are creating intense and unnecessary suffering for yourself.

The Yoga tradition speaks of *dukha*, suffering, and *sukha*, sweetness. Both of these are available to you at any point in life. Satisfying your every desire leads to habit. When you feed the habit, rather than constrain it, the habit becomes compulsion. When you are in the depths of compulsion and addiction, you lose the power to turn away from dukha. The ego will drag you through immense suffering while your truest self is waiting patiently for you to turn toward sukha. You possess the choice to turn in a new direction, away from ego and the old ways of suffering and toward the sweetness and wonder of life. It requires a shift in attitude and your surrender—in other words, engaging your spiritual will.

Surrendering will allow you to move into life and use your spiritual will. Explore and release old feelings. Let go of looking good. Each time discomfort comes up, step back and be a witness. Recognize your feelings and your humanness. Do not take yourself too seriously. Laugh at yourself and be willing to be a beginner at any time. Challenge yourself to move through and beyond feelings of fear, insecurity, inadequacy, and imperfection.

RELATIONSHIPS

One way to identify the source of your challenges with eating and consumption is to observe how you approach relationships. The two are directly linked. One definition of "relationship" is listening to and being present in a dynamic interactive process with something, whether it is yourself, others, or nature. If you look closely, you will realize that unconsciousness, samskara, and other outside influences can all play a role in how you approach your relationships.

YOUR RELATIONSHIP WITH YOURSELF

When you lack a relationship with your higher self, you experience confusion, disconnection from feelings, lack of trust, and loneliness. Not allowing yourself to feel, release, and heal as feelings come up makes life seem overwhelming.

The haste, apparent urgency, avoidance, and fear in daily living fuels disconnection from yourself. It becomes easy to act in harmful ways toward yourself and others. You may forget who you truly are. I experienced this after working in a large corporation for a number of years. I woke up one morning and did not recognize myself. My daily living had nothing to do with my priorities in life. I experienced serious health problems from years of overworking and not living in my truth. I had many opinions, but I did not know how I truly felt about anything. I was following the status quo and ignoring my feelings in order to continue making money and "succeed." I covered up my discontent by living from one vacation to the next. My sense of true power as a human being was lost.

YOUR RELATIONSHIP WITH OTHERS

You may be unaware of the true nature of how you relate to yourself and others. When challenges come up, do you find yourself having problems in relationships?

You would not consciously participate in behaviors that hurt you and others. Unconsciousness accumulates to feed the ego and the resultant coping mechanisms that cover your fears. Codependency is one of these coping mechanisms; doing for others what they need to do for themselves with the illusion of control or desire for recognition. Codependent caretaking is unconsciousness that causes pain and keeps others from being responsible for their own lives. A healthy adult child who continues to live at home because a parent is willing to cook and care for him will not develop self-confidence. A wife who eats pepperoni and mushrooms on pizza, when those items make her ill, develops resentment toward her husband who wants her to eat what he eats. This is harmful to all involved.

The underlying fear of losing something you possess or the fear of not getting what you want drives these behaviors. Remember, fears are a creation of your mind. With appropriate practices, you can stop reverting to unconscious patterns. You cannot make your misperceptions into truth. Eventually you must choose to heal the disconnection or suffer greatly.

YOUR RELATIONSHIP WITH NATURE

Spending conscious time in nature is a helpful way to learn how to reconnect to yourself. However, it can be difficult if you are not accustomed to it. What is your connection to nature? Do you view it from afar rather than going out in it? When you are in nature, do you still see yourself as separate from it? This feeling of separation cultivates fears, such as the fear of animals, plants, and weather.

You may only feel a sense of nature by looking at it in books, on television, and in movies. Indulgence in these activities seems enjoyable but leads to fantasy thinking and more disconnection. Overworking, watching television and movies, spending hours at the computer, and fast-paced living all contribute to a separation from reality. The illusions grow, and the true sense of yourself lessens, until the void or pain seems enormous. Life becomes about running away from internal pain.

I once lived in the foothills of the Sierra Mountains in northern California. It was a beautiful place with a wonderful climate. I thought I admired the nature around me. Yet I worked long hours and was rarely outside. In my mind, I justified overworking because I needed to in order to stay living in that area. Eventually I became miserable—the fantasy of being in nature was not real. I felt very disconnected. Taking the first step to reconnect with nature and myself was uncomfortable. Once I did, the following steps came easier.

Your relationship with the divine

Today's culture encourages compartmentalized living. Changing how you behave according to who is around or where you are is compartmentalizing when it goes against your truth. Compartmentalizing life may help you avoid conflict but will not help you live a fulfilled life. I am not saying that you may not wear different masks for different parts of life. Simply ask yourself if you are consciously choosing your life, or if you are feeling victimized or inadequate. Are you living in conflict with your truth? This feeds disconnection from your sacred self, or the Divine.

You may currently engage in a specific spiritual practice that allows you to feel connected. Or, you may experience a sense of the Divine in your church or rituals. Do you apply the spiritual principles in all aspects of your life, including your car repairs, mortgage payment, income taxes, job, or the performance of other daily responsibilities? What would it take to make this connection in all that you do?

There are many spiritual techniques and resources to draw upon. Perhaps there are too many choices available these days; the overload of information encourages distraction and shallow living. The education system has taught that filling and utilizing the intellect will bring success. In this area, perhaps less is better.

I am not saying don't utilize the intellect; rather, strengthen it as a tool and not as the master of your being. Instead, let your inner knowing, intuition—the higher intellect—guide you. Focus and go deeply with a few simple tools, such as those provided later in this book. Let them bring you results through practice.

Adding to your tools and practices because you think more is better will only dilute your progress. Your lower intellect is concerned with data collection and will continually want more to feed the ego. In modern culture, immersion in external stimuli, including spiritual rules and rituals, has become common. Looking good and doing it right are the priority. This may not be your truth or touch the deepest part of you. A new process, method, or ritual looks good and seems like a savior at first, but eventually leads you to the same place with the same results.

Many spiritual traditions tell a story about a fellow who is looking for the best place to dig a well for water. He follows information from people and things around him and does not give his attention to his intuition. As a result, he digs many shallow holes and ends up without a well that produces water. He realizes that if he had continued to dig in the first location he chose, he would already have water. Choose your approach, check it for accuracy periodically with a teacher or guide, be aware of your experience, and keep going. You will find the flowing well right inside of you. Keep turning inward for your answers. They are all there.

YOUR RELATIONSHIP WITH YOUR INNER CHILD

Like everyone, I have many childhood memories that involve food—both pleasant and unpleasant. The food I ate growing up was very limited and not particularly interesting. I did not like the packaged meats that constituted a significant component of my diet; I felt bad after eating them. Many foods made me feel sick and sluggish, but I did not understand why. Now I know that these foods were heavily processed and my digestion was weak. Most contained chemicals not meant for the human body to process. My family criticized me for being "picky" and "too sensitive." Digestion for me in all parts of life, the inside and the outside, was difficult. I did not eat a lightly cooked, fresh vegetable until I was in my early twenties.

Eating and consumption is often about pleasing the "kid" part of you that is distraught, frightened, and angry. Trying to please the kid part of you may be the impetus for overeating, under-eating, or eating too many times in a day. If you feel this could be happening with you, notice how and what you say aloud and to yourself about food and drink before, during, and after consuming it. Often baby talk or a childish voice will show up. Your tone of voice and posture are good indicators of where your actions are coming from. If you suspect this is happening but are not sure, ask a trusted friend if they hear baby talk or a childish voice from you at times. It takes courage to address these behaviors, but the benefits are large. The conversation may also bring a new level of intimacy to your relationship with your friend.

Communicating with your inner child or the kid part of you, on a regular basis in a clear and concise manner will help you live as a mature adult. It will help you connect with your own nature and do things in your best interest rather than things chosen by an emotionally immature aspect of yourself. There are simple steps that can take you in this direction.

First, acknowledge the reality of your current situation. Gentle, considerate conversation with your inner child, prayer, and kindly caring for the physical body cultivates balance and harmony in all areas of your living. Developing a relationship with your inner child happens by speaking or writing to your inner child. Let him or her know that all is well and that you will consider him or her when making decisions. As you do so, your inner child will begin to develop trust. These steps may feel uncomfortable or even silly at first. If you know the kid part of you is disturbed, setting your intention to listen, support, and love this part of you will make a difference. It may require acting as if you feel loving and supportive for a while until you experience the truth for yourself.

Your relationship with your community

Food can be a beautiful way of connecting to self and others. Most traditional events where people come together involve food and drink. Gathering together to share food is a natural act. Learn to be aware of the effect it has on you. Realize that the food you eat has a significant effect on your ability to be aware. Awareness of self and others is an integral component of being in community.

More and more today, the presence of food and drink is a delusional effort to create some connection between people. People "do lunch" or serve trendy foods to lend credibility to an otherwise empty social event. Disconnection from yourself and lack of intimacy with others cannot be solved with food and drink.

The media has traditionally portrayed the family dinner table with huge smiles. My family sat down to dinner most evenings trying to be the "perfect" family. However, tension was the main course. It was overbearing. Coming together at the dining table is potentially a very intimate activity. Unfortunately, the dining table is sometimes a place for confrontation, anger, isolation, or unresolved feelings.

Many gatherings use food to create pleasure with no concern for health or well-being. The conversation before the meal is about the food, how much it cost, what is in it, how difficult it was to prepare, and how fattening the meal is. During the meal, the conversation is about how good it tastes and about eating too much. The conversation after the meal is about having eaten too much and feeling too full. Very little, if any, intimacy happens. Fulfilling desires in a mechanical unconscious manner does not satisfy your deeper levels of being. After the effects of overeating pass, emptiness on all levels is prevalent, leaving a space for obsessions and cravings.

The sacred nature of most important events, such as weddings, birthdays, and holidays, revolve around food and drink. The result can be bonding among people. From the deepest place within you, realize you have a natural desire to connect with others and nature. In *The Living Bread*, Thomas Merton said, "The mere act of eating together, quite apart from a banquet or some other festival occasion, is by its very nature a sign of friendship and of communion. In modern times we have lost sight of the fact that even the most ordinary actions of our everyday life are invested, by their very nature, with a deep spiritual meaning."

An unconscious attitude toward consumption reduces your chances of connecting to others and to your higher self. It leads to depression, indigestion, and overeating.

With a conscious connection to yourself and to the prana in the food and drink you are consuming, you will begin to experience more depth in your life.

EXPLORING YOUR BELIEFS

Samskara, media influences, your level of consciousness, and how you approach relationships all culminate in a set of beliefs that dictate how you interact with your higher self and with others. You may be conscious of some beliefs but also hold many that are out of your immediate awareness, in the subconscious and unconscious levels. When your behavior comes from beliefs not in your consciousness, trust and honesty with yourself and others are difficult if not impossible. In this case, denial becomes paramount in dealing with life. You often take more than you really need and are unaware of what you are doing. This state of disconnection remains until something significantly painful happens.

Pain is often necessary to initiate the process of examining and making conscious choices about the beliefs driving your behavior. Disconnection from self leads to unconscious, selfish, and self-centered behavior. Often these beliefs are inaccurate perceptions about yourself and your world. Examples of these perceptions are:

- If I am not doing something, I am not worthwhile.
- I am not important.
- I am unique.
- I am different or separate from everyone else.
- What is wrong with them?
- What is wrong with me?
- Nobody really cares about me.
- I have no choice.
- I don't care.
- I deserve this because I was good.
- I have to make things happen.
- I have to figure it out.
- Everyone does it this way.

Make a list of your beliefs and review it with a trusted person. See how many of the items on your list are and are not based in reality. True and clear perception is the basis for knowledge, and knowing is the affirmation of truth. Those beliefs not based in truth are from the distorted perceptions of your mind. These distorted perceptions are having a dramatic effect on your life.

Ask yourself who you are as a being, or spirit, in this body. No matter what your beliefs may be, acknowledge the gift of your body. Regard it highly. Many people carry negative attitudes toward their body. These attitudes cause disturbance in the digestion of food and the digestion of life. "Poor me, why did I get such a bad deal" or "No one understands my problems, I am different" are two common modes of thinking around food and consumption.

Are you willing to give up the old identity? Are you willing to give up your investment in that identity? Are you getting attention from others or separating yourself from them? Are you fueling addiction or consider yourself "special"? Write down how you feel about your eating and relationship to food. This is your starting point today. Accept your starting point. Real and lasting change is not possible until you do.

Consider the saying "What you perceive you believe and what you believe you are." Developing an attitude of acceptance toward your body will allow in the wonder and beauty of life and the life force in the food you eat. Food provides nutrition on the physical, mental, and spiritual levels.

Modern culture espouses a mechanical attitude toward the body and eating. As commercialization has grown, the individual sense of self, connection to nature, and connection to the Divine presence has diminished. People expect the body to behave as desired, and when it does not, disappointment, anger, and depression is the response. Learn to go inside and use simple tools provided later in this book to help shift this attitude toward your body. You can become more loving and nurturing. You will be more compassionate toward yourself and then toward others. Here is a simple tool to help you get started.

First, pause. Make a list of desires for your body. Next, make a list of the expectations you possess about achieving those desires. Then, make a list of your current beliefs about your body. Be as honest as you can be. These lists are for you, not for impressing anyone else.

Your beliefs will dictate what you create. They, along with your desires, will create your reality. Your expectations and attachments to your desires will bring you suffering. The way to make changes is with discipline, practice, and nonattachment.

Be willing to let go of expectations and accept your body as it is right now. Work with it in concert with nature, recognizing the gift of your body in this lifetime. Now the possibilities are immense. How you feel in your body will transform in amazing ways as you open up to your deepest truth.

Most people experience some negative situations in life that affect their consumption. Situations involving abuse, control, anger, and anxiety can be very disturbing to eating patterns. You may feel a victim of culture or your heritage. You do things in certain ways because, "That is how I was brought up." This is the unconscious path.

You can stop allowing those situations to control you. When you raise your consciousness around consumption, you can choose to keep the parts of your upbringing or culture that validate your truth and let the rest go. You can begin to make these changes by exploring your beliefs. Be willing to let go of the negativity, and it will diminish and eventually be gone. Acknowledge the part of you that may not want to let go. Be honest with yourself, let go when you are ready, and the change will come about.

Make a list of the behaviors that you consider problematic. For each one, ask yourself "What belief is behind or driving this behavior? What decision did I make at some point in life to establish this belief?" Some of your beliefs may be from your heritage or upbringing. Some are of your own making.

Examples of beliefs that may or may not hold truth are:

- I have to have coffee or tea to get going in the morning.
- Celebrations are nothing without the cake and ice cream.
- Desserts without white sugar are not dessert.

- I have to have chips with my sandwich.
- Eat more salt when you are in the heat.
- Fish are not animals or meat.
- Vegetables give me gas.
- Green tea is good for everyone, even babies.
- My allergies are environmental, not food related.
- Drinking wine every day is healthy.
- I cannot be strong unless I eat meat or lots of protein.
- Soy products make a man feminine.
- A big glass of cold milk with a meal is wholesome and good for you.
- Carbohydrates are bad.
- Fat is bad; no-fat diets are best.
- The food I eat has nothing to do with body odor or bad breath.
- I can take vitamins instead of eating well.
- Garlic is good for me, and more is better.
- If I substitute fries for salad I am "bad."
- Chai gives me energy; it only has a little caffeine.

Now, ask yourself if you would like to change any of your beliefs. If you are willing to make a change, then next to the old belief write a new approach you would like to cultivate. Subsequently, focus your attention on the new approach and notice the resulting behaviors. It means you must be open to new possibilities.

Look at your entire list. Group the items that are obviously similar together. See where these old beliefs contribute to significant repeating patterns in your life. They may relate to fear, control, or avoidance, among other possibilities. For example, weight loss and/or gain is "being good." This implies a reward mentality, implying who you are relies on your being "good" or "bad." This belief lacks the consideration of who you truly are as an eternal spirit.

Consider the belief that holidays require overeating. What would happen if you approached the holiday simply with a grateful attitude for the wonderful food and love in your life? You could prepare a beautiful, tasty meal that is in the best interest of you, your family, and guests to celebrate the holiday. Show appreciation to everything and everyone without consuming excessive amounts of certain foods because you are "supposed to." You can make any meal a feast with an appreciative attitude, prana-filled food, sincere presentation, and conscious eating.

Choose your food by what your body needs and not just what the tongue wants. In your list of new approaches, for example, you can validate your connection to self by choosing vegetables and fruits that are in your best interest. This approach has nothing to do with being good or bad; it reflects a response to your actual experience. Learn to eat without a rigid attitude and with validation of your own experience. This will help you undo the samskara, and the change will translate into all areas of your life. Connect how you feel in your body with what you ate, validating your choice. If you continually question your approach to eating, your attention and energy will run all over the place, depleting you. Validating your process is important.

Another step in this process of change is to soften your likes and dislikes so that you may begin to see the range of possibilities in living. Strong likes and dislikes generate from your beliefs and impressions. They are tools of the ego. Identify the samskara that is beneath your strong like or dislike and bring your awareness to it in order to move beyond it and heal. Focus on your new attitude and your likes and dislikes will begin to soften. Practice neutrality and detachment toward your food and all possessions. If you don't feel neutral or detached, ask yourself what would happen if you did feel that way. Then, act as if you *do* feel neutral or detached. See what happens.

Cultivate an attitude of knowing all is well. Realize that abundance is available to you in all areas of life. The strong likes and dislikes are based in fear of the unknown, fear of there not being enough, or fear of not getting what you want. When you become clear in your connection to self, there is no need to hoard or push things away based on likes and dislikes.

Your relationship with food, yourself, and others will flow more easily and deepen over time. Learn to pause and be a witness, rather than a judge, to your own feelings and behaviors. Learn to be the witness or observer of your mind. Keep a sense of humor.

The mind is merely a tool to provide experience and liberation for the soul. Awareness works through the mind. Be willing to giggle at yourself. Enjoy being human. Why not enjoy yourself? Explore the beliefs that drive your answer to this last question. You may decide to change some of those beliefs.

Some activities of the mind keep you from enjoying life. Your mind may tell you that you need to react to feelings. Remember, just because you feel a feeling does not mean you need to act on it and often the feeling is not correct. It also doesn't mean you *are* that feeling. If you swallow the feeling, you will continue to carry it around. Let it go and the energy will move and disperse.

Let go of the fears of eating too much, weighing too much, or being imperfect. Learn to connect how you feel after you eat something to making the choice about what you put into your mouth. This is a huge step in emotional maturity and elevating your consciousness. It requires:

- Facing reality—awareness,
- Practice,
- An attitude of adventure and creativity,
- Merging your senses with your world, like a child or an animal does naturally,
- Engaging your enthusiasm in a playful way.

Learning to engage your senses consciously and to listen to your body's responses is a path to happiness. Become a nonjudgmental observer of yourself and free yourself from suffering. Nonjudgmental observation is key to finding your truth. Writing down your observations is a helpful way to see the total picture of what is happening in your life. Use the Wellness Journal in Appendix B to help you begin this nonjudgmental observation.

Beginning this daring journey in the area of food and consumption can open many doors for spiritual growth. The use of journaling, affirmations of the present, breath work, prayer, and meditation will bring clarity and attitude adjustment. Prayers and devotion around food preparation and consumption are a simple place to start. Suggestions are available later in this book.

New Ways to Relate to Food

PRINCIPLES OF AYURVEDA

Ayurveda is an organic nature based approach to living that brings clarity and depth. Since it has a dramatically different basis than modern living, you will assimilate it best when you take it in small steps.

Ayurveda views the entire cosmos as made up of the five elements of earth, water, fire, air, and ether. These elements group into the *doshas*, which represent the basic functions in everyone and everything. There are three doshas: *vata*, *pitta*, and *kapha*. These doshas, or organizing forces, make up your individual constitution. In other words, you consist of the above-mentioned five elements and you connect to the cosmos through these elements.

Ideally, the food you eat includes the six tastes. These tastes have a variety of twenty qualities such as heavy or light and rough or smooth. Through these qualities, the elements connect to the tastes, and the tastes to the doshas. This connection shows how what you eat and how you eat it affects your well-being. The six tastes are discussed in more detail in the section Ayurvedic Food Classification.

In Ayurveda, the energies that existed at the time of your conception and birth make up your *prakruti*, your unique constitution, in its natural state. As was mentioned, the elements of nature (earth, fire, water, air, ether) come together to form the doshas. Your prakruti is your unique combination of these three doshas. People have all three doshas within them.

You can send your life out of balance at any point in time based on how you conduct and treat yourself. Meaning, the vata, pitta, and kapha forces within you go out of balance. This out-of-balance condition is your *vikruti*, the current state of your being. You can be out of balance for so long that the vikruti seems like your prakruti. That is, you mistake the out-of-balance condition for your natural state of being.

The following information about each dosha will help you begin to develop a better understanding of how to best balance your constitution.

Vata relates primarily to the elements of air and ether and the energy of movement. Vata directs breathing, muscle movement, heartbeat, and cellular activity. Light, dry, cold, rough, clear, subtle, and mobile are vata characteristics. When vata is out of balance, you may experience fear, anxiety, and twitching movements. Vata is creative and flexible when balanced.

Pitta relates primarily to the fire and water elements and the energy of digestion and transformation. Pitta directs body temperature, digestion, absorption, assimilation, and metabolism. Hot, sharp, light, oily, liquid, and mobile are pitta characteristics. When pitta is out of balance, you may experience anger, jealousy, inflammation, and hatred. Pitta is intelligent, understanding, and manifests things easily when in balance.

Kapha relates primarily to the earth and water elements and the energy of lubrication. Kapha directs the water supply in the body, lubricates joints, keeps skin moist, and supports the immune system. Heavy, slow, oily, liquid, cold, dense, soft, smooth, and sticky are kapha characteristics. When kapha is out of balance, you may experience greed, attachment, hoarding, and congestion. Kapha is calm, loving, and forgiving when in balance.

One more significant component for attaining balance in your system is the *agni*, digestive fire, available within you. The energy that is required to digest, absorb, distribute, and eliminate what you eat and drink is agni. It includes the enzymes and metabolic processes of digestion. Your metabolism is a result of the state of your agni.

You either fuel or reduce agni by what and how you eat. If your digestive fire is low, there is not enough energy available to transform food into something useful to your body or mind. Physical signs of reduced agni are gas, burping, belching, slow digestion, little to no perspiration, difficulty waking up in the morning, and constipation. Signs of too much agni also include burping and belching, but a burning feeling in the upper digestive tract is more common. Other symptoms of excess agni are diarrhea, irritability, and excessive talking.

The condition of each of your body systems is dependent on agni, including digestion, clarity, mental well-being, and how you feel in general. When agni is balanced, food is transformed through digestion into consciousness at the cellular and body levels. When agni is imbalanced, food is transformed into toxins. The accumulation of toxins results in disease.

Learning to understand your constitution frees you to acknowledge and begin meeting your individual needs. Your individual constitution has certain physical, mental, and emotional characteristics. This approach to working with your body, mind, and spirit leads to balance, harmony, peace of mind, and a greater opportunity for health and well-being. The ideal way to determine your constitution is to utilize the assistance of an experienced Ayurvedic practitioner, but you can get started in making changes toward balance by answering the following questionnaire to assess your constitution.

WHAT IS YOUR CONSTITUTION? (DOSHA QUIZ)

Make two copies of the survey below. Fill out the first copy by putting a check mark next to characteristics you identify with throughout your life. The second time through answer the questions based on how you feel now and in the last couple of months. The first will represent your prakruti, your unique characteristics at your conception and the second is your vikruti, or your current condition. Your answers on both copies could be the same.

Total the number of checks under each of the doshas: vata, pitta, and kapha. One dosha is often dominant, but it could be that two are equal in the number of checks. A small number of people will have the same number of checks for all three doshas. Then, look at your totals in terms of their ratio relative to one another. For example, V15, P10, and K5, would be V3, P2, and K1.

	Vata	**Pitta**	**Kapha**
Body type	thin	medium	large
Weight	lighter	medium	heavy
Hair	dry, brown, black, brittle, thin, knotted, curly	straight, oily, blonde, gray, red, balding, wavy	thick, oily, lustrous, any color
Skin	dry, thin, cool, darker	oily, smooth, warm, pinkish	thick, cool, pale
Nails	dry, brittle, break easily	flexible, pink, healthy	thick, smooth, oily
Eyes	small, active, dry, sunken black, brown	sharp, bright, sensitive to light, gray, green, pale blue	large, calm, loving, brown, blue
Nose	uneven	long, pointed	short, round
Lips	dry, crack easily, black or brownish	inflame easily, red, yellowish	smooth, oily, whitish
Teeth	large, protruding, thin gums	medium, sensitive gums	white, strong gums
Chin	thin, sharp	medium taper	rounded, double
Cheeks	sunken, wrinkled	smooth, straight	round, plump

Neck	tall, thin	medium	large
Chest	sunken, flat	medium	round, large
Belly	flat, sunken	medium	large, pot belly
Hips	narrow, thin	medium	large, heavy
Joints	cold, cracking	medium	large, lubricated
Appetite	irregular	strong	slow, steady
Digestion	irregular, gassy	quick, burning	prolonged, mucous
Taste (healthy)	sweet, sour, salty	sweet, bitter, astringent	bitter, pungent, astringent
Thirst	variable	plenty	sparse
Elimination	constipation	loose	sluggish, oily
Sex drive	intense, steady	variable	moderate
Physical activity	hyperactive	moderate	sedentary
Mental activity	quick, constant	moderate	slow, dull
Emotions	fear, uncertain, flexible	anger, jealous, determined	attachment, greed, calm
Faith	variable, changing	intense, extreme	deep, consistent, mellow
Financial	spends on trivial items	spends on luxuries	preserves assets
Intellect	quick, may be faulty	accurate response	slow, precise

Recollection	recent good, remote poor	distinct	slow, sustained
Sleep	irregular, sleeplessness	little and sound	deep, prolonged
Speech	quick, unclear	sharp, penetrating	slow, monotone

Total check marks for each dosha: Vata___, Pitta___, Kapha___.

Place them in a ratio with the highest first and lowest last. From this, you can determine your predominant dosha(s). Asking a close friend or family member to give their perspective on some of your characteristics can be an interesting exercise. This can be helpful in gaining clarity about how others experience you in life—particularly if it does not match your view of yourself.

Create a balanced and harmonious life by learning the relationship between the doshas and your body and mind. It will naturally assist you to enhance your relationship with what you consume and with all of nature.

If it seems complicated at first, it will get easier with practice. This view of yourself and living in the world may be very different from your current view. If it all seems like too much, gradually select the tools you can work with and let them produce excellent results in your life. I hope this inspires you to learn more about Ayurveda as a way of life.

CONSCIOUS CONSUMPTION

Perhaps you really want to bring new depth into your life and move beyond unconsciousness and obsession with eating and drinking. First, recognize that change is a process. Take small steps in the direction you want to go.

Let go of performance orientation and feeling compelled to do everything at once. Let go of perfectionism, it will reduce your ego.

Bring consciousness to your behavior in all areas of life, particularly to anything you put in and on your body. Consciousness around food and your relationship to it provides you the opportunity to choose foods that are in your best interest, not just to please others, to look good, or to "do it right."

Your body and mind are your tools for this life. You are not your mind. You are not your body. You are not your thoughts. Your attitude and your choices dictate the condition of your mind. In other words, what you eat and consume on all levels affects how your mind operates.

Poor mental and physical health does not need to be a permanent condition. You train your mind by what you expose it to each day. Weakness and low energy are the natural consequence of foods and attitudes that perpetuate disconnection. Practicing honesty, particularly with yourself, reestablishes the connection to your innermost self.

Consider the saying, "You are what you eat."

What you consume on all levels goes into your subconscious mind. It then dictates your attitude, mood, self-image, and reactions to life. Learning to engage your senses and to listen to your body's responses is an amazing adventure. Conscious living is the product of what you feed your mind. Your mind dictates how you lead your life. Therefore, you dictate the strength of your mind by what you feed it. When you allow it to fall into habits that do not serve you, you suffer. Consider the saying that: "pain is part of life and suffering is a choice." Painful things happen in life. Loved ones pass on, possessions come and go, relationships end. Everything is changing except that which is eternal in you. Get to know that unchanging part of you. It is pure love.

Consider that your eternal spirit connects to the body through the endocrine (hormone) system. Specific scientific studies show that focusing your thoughts on gratitude, joy, love, and consciousness increases the hormone flow from the pituitary gland in the body.

This increased hormone flow is said to open up the brain, flowing through to the pineal gland. The increased hormone flow to the pineal gland expands thought frequencies that raise the frequency of your aura or the energy field around your body. This makes it possible to bring in higher frequencies of thinking to continue the cycle.

Responsible consumption is a distinct component of spiritual growth.

Many spiritual traditions suggest going inside and connecting to your innermost or higher self. Most suggest learning to live from there. Reading or listening to someone talk about spirituality may be an intellectually fascinating event, yet it can be difficult to incorporate into daily living.

Practicing a spiritual approach in daily life requires a change of beliefs, a change in attitudes, and some courage to get started. Once you get started, it takes courage and discipline to continue living in a conscious manner. It means saying "no thanks" to many things so that you can focus wholeheartedly on what is important to you. The steps to change beliefs and attitudes are essential. Avoiding the underlying beliefs and looking only at the surface of life creates stagnation, boredom, discontent, and toxicity.

By focusing your attention, you will increase your awareness. Use this awareness to reduce and eliminate the old impressions in your cellular memory. Awareness does not mean alertness. Alertness implies effort and tension. Being aware is being alert without tension and strain. From a relaxed state of awareness, you can experience true spontaneity. Life becomes more interesting and commitment is easier.

Give your attention to your own experience rather than something outside of you. Learn to read your own energy and observe when you are stuck in fear or an impression from the past. This will help you distinguish the difference between projecting from your past and having a current experience—even with food and eating. The results may not look as you expect. Allow the possibilities to blossom beyond your ego and limited thinking.

Eating is a vital part of the art of living. Harmonious and balanced eating is one of the keys to a long, healthy life. It promotes sukha, the sweetness in life. Conscious eating begins with your attitude. If you want to find peace, harmony, and a sense of self, eat and drink the purest foods possible. Be clear that what you are consuming is really nourishing for your body, mind, and soul, and then allow in the prana.

Keep things simple, let go of old programming and beliefs, and allow in a new perspective based simply in nature. Learn to live and eat in a way that works for your well-being and you will move beyond cravings, addictions, and rigidity. Practice awareness and making appropriate choices for you in the moment. These are practical skills for transforming your life around food and drink.

Engaging the connection to the food and drink you consume will raise your consciousness on all levels, physical, mental, and spiritual. Addressing the emotional aspects of your eating is a critical component to making real changes. Incorporating your spiritual nature into your consumption will enrich your life.

CLARIFY YOUR PRIORITIES

In a recent newspaper article, the author said, "I wish I had the time, space, knowledge and resources to grow my own vegetables, make my own bread, and gather eggs from my own chickens. I wish I had the time and money to shop exclusively at farmers' markets and organic food stores. But modern life doesn't permit many of us the luxury to be the perfect local, organic consumer."[2] This statement is a good example of feeling trapped by living and the thinking that "more is better" and "if I don't do it perfectly, then why bother doing any of it."

The article's author did offer some great solutions, such as:

- Be informed.
- Read labels.
- Talk to farmers.
- Talk to produce managers.
- Buy locally when available.
- Buy organic when available.
- Grow what you can, even a sprig of basil to add to your spaghetti.
- Trade your mangoes for your neighbor's avocados.

All of these are significant steps in the direction of balance and harmony. Each will make a difference in your life and the lives of others. However, going beyond the attitude of being a victim of society is where real and lasting change comes about.

Realize that the first step leads to the next. Movement in the direction you would like to go is enough of a start. Each step makes a difference in your energy and the energy on this planet. You are a part of all that is.

Make a list of the top 5 priorities in your life. Review it regularly (e.g., monthly or quarterly) to see if you are living your priorities.

Are you saying yes when you want to say no? Do you find yourself saying no when you would like to be saying yes? Adjust the list for significant changes in life so that the list reflects your true priorities. If you are doing things that are not in your priorities, eliminate them in order to regain your focus. Satisfaction and acceptance come out of this process. When bombarded with requests and opportunities, the list is a good tool to prevent distraction. Be sure to allow time for "doing nothing."

Clarity and simplicity regarding your priorities will help you see how you turn away from what you really want because your life is full of other things. For example, be clear that having simple, fresh food in your life is a priority. Set your intention to prepare food at home most days and allow the time in your schedule for regular shopping. If these necessary activities tend to be pushed aside, they need to be clearly stated in your priorities and reorganized in your thinking. Food and eating are a foundation of living rather than an incidental after thought.

Learn to be aware of and take responsibility for what you buy and what you consume.

Identify the necessary changes in your consumption. If you are shopping and feel confused, pause and ground yourself to the center of the planet. Do not purchase anything without finding your clarity. Sometimes the best thing is to stop shopping without buying. When I think I need something new, I wait two weeks to see if I still think I really need it. If so, then I shop for it. Often the need disappears.

Decide in advance if your shopping is for research or to buy. Do not go to buy food when you are hungry. Take a list with you for shopping so as not to get distracted. Execute a simple, systematic plan with guidelines to support your clarity. Allow a gradual process of change to occur. It will help you develop trust both in the process and in your new connection to self.

As a rule, modern living encourages you to hand the responsibility for your well-being over to something outside of you. For example, health services marketed to make a profit do not have your best interest as the top priority. Large companies in most industries make it their business to satisfy a fast-moving disconnected clientele. Although you may still choose to do business with large companies, select only the things that are in your best interest. Know what you are looking for and stick to it.

Read the labels and examine the contents of anything you are going to use or consume. If you cannot pronounce it or do not recognize it, do not eat or use it until you are clear with yourself. Be willing to say no and look for an alternative. This is an important step in validating yourself. The alternatives are obvious when you are clear about your willingness to be responsible for your decisions. There are many known carcinogens in food, drink, and body products. Most heavily processed foods and foods grown and processed with toxic chemicals have little to no prana. When you consider the price you pay in illness and feeling poorly, how can you not afford to purchase clean, organic products?

Acknowledgement and acceptance of your current reality provides you with a starting point from which real, lasting change can take place.

Practice contentment by accepting wholeheartedly what is. This does not necessarily mean condoning or agreeing, just accepting. The belief that materialism will bring you contentment is prevalent in modern society; however, your attitude and acceptance are what cultivate true contentment, peace, and joy.

You may not be honest with yourself about your place in life. On the other hand, you may be worried about what other people think of you and are allowing such worries to direct your behavior. What or how others think of you is not your business; you have no control over it. Step into your reality. Be the best person you can be today. You are enough. Let the rest go.

Are you doing what you think you are doing, or are you just thinking about it and not actually living it? Be honest with yourself about what is happening. You may be fooling yourself. Accumulating large amounts of information does not amount to much living. Open your mind to something completely different, something that may be out of your current realm of thinking. Take your thinking and approach back-to-nature-based living.

Engage in practical methods that validate who you are. Step away from things that lure you to move faster, work more, or have more. Fast movement gives you less opportunity to hear and to connect to your true inner voice. Slow down to listen, and be aware of your results.

Turning on your consciousness ignites your personal power. Consciousness validates your spirit and brings true joy. When you remain conscious, your day will be pleasant and smooth—even when it does not go as you had planned. You remained connected to your true knowingness.

You will go on as usual if you choose not to be attentive to the connection between what you consume and how you feel. If you keep doing what you are doing, you will keep getting what you have been getting. I recognized this in my own life when enthusiasm for life would come up and then go down so quickly. For years, I drank alcohol in business and social situations. After drinking, I felt depressed for days or weeks but did not make the connection between consuming a depressant and how I felt. When I eliminated alcohol, I was able to work through the beliefs that contributed to feeling the need to drink and the subsequent depression.

Attitudes and thinking either connect you or disconnect you from your true sense of self. The choice is yours. Remember, you can resolve any problem with the connection to your higher self. Take charge of your life now. Learn to use your breath, affirmation of the present, meditation, and prayer to cultivate your connection. Begin this change with food and consumption. Let go of expectations and surrender to the wonder of life. Forgive yourself and others. Practice facing reality and accepting life. Go forward consciously.

Simple Tools for Your New Path

Yoga and Ayurveda are vast, multidimensional, intertwined traditions that remind you to live in tune with nature inside and out. There are many valid methods as well as many gimmicks available today. The following suggestions and tools are from my personal experience and experience working with others. I encourage you to find what works best for you. Seize the opportunity to realize unity of your body, mind, and spirit.

AYURVEDIC FOOD CLASSIFICATION

In Yoga and Ayurveda, everything in nature is organized in three categories called the *mahagunas*. Yoga uses the mahagunas as a tool to understand and master the mind. Ayurveda uses the mahagunas to restore and maintain balance. The mahagunas are *sattva, rajas,* and *tamas*. Sattva is equilibrium or balance, rajas is activity, and tamas is inertia. They are each present within the mind at any one time and are continually changing. How you experience yourself and the world is dictated by which is predominant at any moment.

The practices of Yoga and Ayurveda move you toward balance and clarity, a state of sattva. You will maintain balance, clarity, and contentment no matter what is happening around you. Sattvic living is balanced living that offers freedom in the body and mind. Sattvic living slows the aging process, promoting healthy longevity.

Sattvic foods are pure and balancing. Fresh foods with little, if any, processing are sattvic. In other words, shortening the distance between the moment of harvest and when the food arrives on your plate is ideal. Sattvic foods bring purity and calm to the mind. They promote cheerfulness, peace, and mental clarity. These foods include such things as fresh and dried fruits, fresh fruit juices, whole and sprouted grains, unleavened breads from whole or sprouted grains, lightly cooked vegetables, legumes, nuts, seeds, herbal teas and ghee. Sattvic foods that are suitable for your constitution digest easily. They provide strength, vitality, and increased energy.

Rajasic foods are stimulating and can cause physical and mental stress. Eating rajasic foods overexcites the body and mind and encourages circulatory and nervous system disorders. Foods that are rajasic include garlic, coffee, tea, tobacco, salt, refined sugar, soft drinks, and chocolate among others. These foods create imbalance in the mind, body, spirit connection resulting in a restless, overactive mind. Living primarily a rajasic life demands continuous feeding on strong-tasting foods that are hot, sour, salty, and/or pungent. Eating and drinking in modern culture revolves primarily around rajasic and tamasic foods that contribute significantly to the perceived high stress level.

Tamasic foods are impure, rotten, or dead and produce feelings of heaviness and lethargy. This category includes all types of meat, fish, eggs, drugs, alcohol, overcooked foods, packaged foods, fermented, burned, fried, barbecued, reheated, stale, or those containing preservatives. Eating tamasic foods makes a person dull and lethargic, lacking motivation and purpose. Individuals who eat a tamasic diet like cold, stale, and acrid tastes, tend to be depressed, and suffer from chronic ailments.

Overeating is tamasic, as it results in ama in the body. This is the case no matter what type of food you overeat.

In the beginning, it may require a significant conscious effort to balance your eating. However, your food preferences will continue to alter naturally as you develop a stronger sense of your inner truth.

Using the information in this book, make a list of the foods you choose to eat. Focus on your list. The desire and craving for items not on your list will fall away with lack of attention. The norm is to follow craving and intense desires. When you do this, the mind weakens. The imbalance prompting the craving grows, leading to suffering. Rajas and tamas increase in the mind, increasing the imbalance.

The true nature of the mind is sattva, or even-mindedness. Tamas, or the inert aspect of nature, also brings you sleep, which you need. Rajas supports activity in life. As a healthy, peaceful human being, you can learn to acknowledge and be grateful toward all aspects of nature without having to be rigid about right and wrong. Although you may choose not to consume tamasic foods and to moderate your consumption of rajasic foods, you can still be grateful for all of nature's aspects. Life is a work of art and not black and white. Tamas is not all "bad."

When you consume things in life that take you out of balance, you may develop intense desires, anger, rage, or inflammation. The instability that develops from this condition will drive you to look for ways to "ground," or feel more connected to the earth. Some people think that consuming tamasic foods help them to ground. Actually, the food's inert nature creates a false sense of grounding. The heavy "full" feeling experienced after eating meat is a good example of this. A brief sense of "being okay" occurs and then more imbalance follows. The desire for this heaviness after eating meat often coincides with being "stuck" in the ego. This may be experienced in such things as not admitting wrongs or holding on to mistakes.

Sattvic root vegetables such as carrots, beets, parsnips, turnips, or sweet potatoes are also grounding foods. Eating sattvic foods appropriate for your constitution will increase your sense of balance and well-being.

The following is a list of sattvic foods. Consider what is best for balancing your individual constitution, the strength of your agni, and any imbalance you are currently experiencing. In other words, not all of the foods on this list are best for you right now, but draw from this list to establish an excellent foundation.

Sattvic foods include:

Adzuki beans	Fava beans	Pecans
Almonds	Figs	Pineapple (sweet)
Amaranth	(fresh or dried)	Pine nuts
Apples	Filberts	Pinto beans
Apricots	Flowers	Plums
Artichokes	(edible and	(sweet or sour)
Arugula	sweet)	Pomegranates
(small amounts)	Fruit juices	Prunes
Asparagus	(fresh)	Pumpkin
Bananas	Ghee	Quinoa
Barley	Grapefruits	Raisins
Basmati rice	Grapes	Raspberries
Bean sprouts	Green beans	Rice
(all kinds)	Honeydew	Rutabaga
Beets	Jerusalem	Sesame seeds
Black beans	artichokes	(hulled or
Blackberries	Kale	unhulled)
Black-eyed peas	Kohlrabi	Soybeans
Broccoli	Lentils	Soymilk (fresh)
Brussels sprouts	(black or tan)	Spinach
Buckwheat	Lettuce	Strawberries
Buttermilk (fresh)	Lima beans	Sugar cane (raw)
Cabbage	(small amounts)	Summer squash
(red or green)	Loganberries	Sunflower seeds
Cantaloupe	Macadamia	Sweet potatoes
Carob	nuts	Tangerines
Carrots	Mangoes	(sweet)
Cashews	Maple syrup	Teff
Cauliflower	Milk (fresh, raw,	Turnips
Celery	and pure)	Walnuts
Chard	Millet	(English or black)
	Mother's milk	Watercress

Cherries	Mung beans	Watermelon
(sweet or sour)	(whole or split)	Wheat
Chestnuts	Mustard	Wild rice
Chinese cabbage	greens	Winter squash
Coconut	Oats (steel cut	Yacon
Cornmeal	or berries)	Yams
Cranberries	Oranges (sweet)	Yogurt
Cucumbers	Papayas	(freshly made)
Dates (fresh)	Parsnips	Zucchini
Escarole	Peaches	

Rajasic foods include aged cheeses, avocado, cottage cheese, dried dates, egg, eggplant, all fermented food, bottled fruit juices, garbanzo beans, garlic, guava, ice cream, kidney beans, lime, lemon, red lentils, molasses, olives, peanuts, peanut oil, pepper, pickles, potatoes, pumpkin seeds, radishes, salt (all kinds), sour cream, commercial soy milk, sugar (all kinds), tomatoes, vinegar, yogurt (not freshly made).

Tamas foods include alcohol, animal meat (beef, chicken, fish, fowl, goat, lamb, pork, rabbit, shellfish, turkey, venison), fried foods, frozen foods, onions, leeks, leftovers, margarine, microwaved food, food with preservatives, and mushrooms (all kinds).

THE SIX TASTES

Ayurveda recognizes six different tastes in food: sweet, salty, sour, bitter, pungent, and astringent. These tastes relate to the five elements in nature. They influence the balance of the doshas (vata, pitta, and kapha) in the body. In other words, the amount of each dosha your body produces depends upon the tastes you consume. The tastes also relate to the various human emotions and levels of consciousness. Taste is to the body what emotion is to the mind.

The **sweet** taste is heavy, moist, and cool. Sweetness relates to the earth and water elements. The word sweet in Ayurveda means nourishing to the tissues of the body on all levels. Most nourishing foods are bland or neutral in flavor. Keep in mind that references to the sweet taste in this book are to foods that are nourishing and pleasant, not sugary. Foods like bread, rice, nuts, oils, milk, ripe fruit, carrots, beets, and sweet potatoes have the sweet taste. The sweet taste reduces vata and pitta and increases kapha. It nourishes the body and mind and brings satisfaction. Too much sweet leads to greed.

The **sour** taste is warm, moist, and heavy. Sourness relates to the earth and fire elements. Examples are citrus fruit, cheese, tart apples, and tomatoes. The sour taste reduces vata and increases pitta and kapha. It encourages elimination and improves appetite and digestion. The sour taste encourages external evaluation. Too much sour leads to jealousy and envy.

The **salty** taste is heavy, moist, and warm. Saltiness relates to the water and fire elements. Sea vegetables and soy sauce are good examples. The salty taste reduces vata and increases pitta and kapha. It assists the body to eliminate wastes, softens body tissue, and encourages enthusiasm for life. Too much leads to craving and indulgence in sensory pleasures.

The **pungent** taste is hot, light, and dry. Pungency relates to the air and fire elements. Examples are ginger, hot peppers, radishes, spinach, turnips, and fennel. The pungent taste increases vata and pitta and reduces kapha. It encourages the body to let go of secretions such as milk, semen, and fat and improves appetite. It encourages extroversion and craving for intensity. Too much leads to impatience and anger.

The **bitter** taste is cold, light, and dry. Bitterness relates to the air and ether elements. Examples are leafy greens, endive, eggplant, coffee, and tea. The bitter taste increases vata and reduces pitta and kapha. Purifying and drying, it assists to return all tastes to a normal balance. It also increases appetite and is an anti-aphrodisiac. It leads to dissatisfaction and the desire to change, forcing you to face reality. Too much leads to irritation and bitterness in attitude.

The **astringent** taste is cool, light, and dry. Astringency relates to the air and earth elements. Examples are legumes, cruciferous vegetables, cranberries, potatoes, and rye. The astringent taste increases vata and reduces pitta and kapha. Astringency is healing, purifying, and constricting in the body. It reduces secretions and is an anti-aphrodisiac. It leads to introversion, tending away from stimulation and excitement. Too much introversion leads to anxiety, insecurity, and fear.

Ideally, all of the six tastes would be included in each meal. This does not imply that adding refined sugar and processed salt to food is a good idea. Each of the tastes occurs in nature and can be included in a balanced meal. Depending upon your combination of doshas (whether they are in or out of balance), the condition of your agni, and the season, you will need to emphasize some tastes over others. The tendency when you are out of balance is to crave one or two tastes and forget the others. However, following cravings of just one or two tastes will contribute to further imbalance.

Cravings do not typically represent true hunger. They may be healthy or unhealthy. They may arise from a lack of a nutrient, some underlying pathology—such as a parasite or an allergy—or from suppressed feelings. You can identify which is the cause by listening to your body and its responses in all areas of your life. A craving that arises from a lack of a nutrient indicates an actual need in the body. If the craving is for something not particularly good for you, choose a healthier food than the one you are craving in order to take care of the body's need. For example, if you crave cheese you may need calcium. That can be better satisfied by chewing one teaspoon of raw sesame seeds or by including more hijiki, kale, or broccoli in your eating each day. If you do this, the craving will subside.

When you eliminate or reduce sugar intake, a craving for salt will sometimes come up. Do not follow the craving. The *vipak* or post-digestive effect of the salt is sweet like sugar. Everything you eat has a taste that your tongue picks up, the energy of cold or hot during digestion, and a post-digestive effect.

Foods possess individual qualities. Some foods are cooling and appropriate for summer. Other foods are heating and more appropriate for winter. If you live in an environment with extreme seasons—such as very cold winters—choose locally grown foods as much possible. Select winter vegetables and fruits from the closest locale. Eating cooling tropical fruits during a cold winter may seem exotic and tantalizing, but the fruit is cooling and confusing to your system. It will contribute to imbalance and compromise your well-being. Likewise, eating heating foods such as sesame oil, hot peppers, or alcohol during a hot summer will lead to agitation and inflammation.

For more information about the relationship between the tastes, elements, doshas, food, and your well-being, see Appendix C and D.

IDENTIFYING FOODS FOR YOUR CONSTITUTION

There are many types of food from which to choose for your individual constitution.

If you eat meat, and you are willing to look at what that means, consider the following. The condition of your intestinal flora is critical to your overall health. Animal products putrefy in the colon because they are difficult to digest and move very slowly through the digestive tract. Wholesome food travels more easily through the digestive tract, leaving little time to spoil and incite disease within the body. Fiber absorbs unwanted, excess fats, cleans the intestines, provides bulk, and aids in peristalsis. Most food from plants is high in fiber content; meat, poultry, and dairy products have none.

Meat from animals contains the animal's waste material, including adrenaline and uric and lactic acids. They also contain the energy of the animal at its death, likely fear. Before adding condiments, the primary contributors to the flavor of a hamburger are the blood and urine of the cow. The average meat eater consumes large amounts of protein; the resulting excess of nitrogen in the blood creates many long-term health problems. Increasing one's risk of developing a degenerative disease means decreasing ones chance to live a naturally long, healthy life. People with large centenarian populations eat very little animal flesh. In general, Ayurveda suggests a balanced diet without meats.

One of the most common questions I receive is, "What about protein?" I suggest not worrying about it. Instead, focus on eating in a balanced way and there will be enough. The need for protein in modern culture is perhaps misunderstood and exaggerated. If you are consuming foods that are lowering your energy, such as refined sugar and foods heavily processed with sugar and salt, a larger dose of protein may give you a boost temporarily. When you continue to take in larger amounts of protein, however, it accumulates in your system as ama, leading to disease. Eventually, you will become sluggish and feel heavy again. Then begins the cycle of looking for some way to fix it, missing the cause altogether.

Since it is not a black-and-white approach, there may be an occasion when an imbalance is so extreme that a meat product such as fish may be necessary for a temporary period. If you are transitioning away from animal flesh, it will be helpful to talk with others who have made this change. Gradual change is a good approach for many people, and some people are successful at just stopping one day. The most important thing is to understand and focus on a balanced approach to eating for yourself.

The following are lists of some of the most nourishing foods for balancing each of the doshas. Lists of this nature may vary in different books. If a food you like to eat is not on the list, you might consider leaving it out of your eating to see how you feel without it. The types of foods discussed here include whole grains, legumes, beans and peas, sea vegetables, fresh vegetables, dairy, fresh condiments, ghee, unrefined and natural sugars, spices, and herbs.

Depending on your combination of doshas, you may draw foods from two of these lists, shifting the emphasis with the change of season. For example if you are primarily pitta and vata doshas, you may emphasize more pitta-balancing foods in summer and vata-balancing foods in winter. In the beginning, work with the lists; consider the strength of your agni and the season. Emphasize what is grown locally and cleanly. Observe your results. Continue to refine your choices based on your experience.

Balancing any of the doshas will benefit from avoiding caffeine, alcohol, saturated fats, excess salt, extreme use of spices, fried foods, hot spicy foods, highly processed foods, yeast, meat, ice cream, peanuts, refined sugar, and stale or old food. Eliminating these items from your eating will improve how you feel quickly. You may experience some withdrawal and detoxification as your body responds to the change.

Eliminate or minimize frozen and canned foods, commercial preparations, and any food with ingredients that are unknown to you. In all cases, use fresh, organic, biodynamic or unsprayed, locally grown produce that is in season. Focus on the list of best choices for you rather than items to avoid.

Balancing the doshas is an art of living consciously with your unique constitution and the condition of your agni at any point in time. When a particular dosha is out of balance, there will be symptoms as mentioned previously. Eat foods that will balance that dosha to help eliminate the symptoms. When your agni is weak, eat simple, easily digested foods that are balancing for you. When the agni is very weak, such as with a cold, some heavy foods that are normally okay for you may not be.

Observe which foods are easy for you to digest and which are more challenging. For example, you may typically digest adzuki beans or cottage cheese easily, but with a cold, they may be too much work for your system. Avoid them for a while and allow your agni to strengthen.

In general, for all doshas, eat foods in their most natural state. Eating on a regular schedule in a relaxed, calm environment is important. Avoid food that is pretending to be something it is not. Eating tofu and calling it some kind of meat is not facing reality. Playing with the mind and not facing reality will increase unconsciousness.

For all doshas, eating yeast bread disturbs digestion, particularly when eaten daily. If you are going to eat baked goods, try flat breads and muffins without yeast, baking soda, baking powder or refined sugar. A simple delicious recipe for muffins is available in Appendix A. Naturally dried fruits and vegetables are a reasonable alternative when fresh are not available. Avoid the tendency to overeat dried fruits and nuts, as they seem so small. Overeating nuts and/or dried fruits disturbs agni, leading to many imbalances in your system. Reconstitute dried foods for easier digestion. This may also help prevent overeating.

As you read the following lists, notice the items that you have naturally gravitated toward that are balancing for your constitution.

VATA FOODS

Vata remains in balance with foods that are warm, cooked well, oily, soupy, and are easiest to digest.

- Grains such as basmati rice (brown and white), wild rice, sushi rice, oats, bulgar wheat, amaranth, and barley are ideal. Small amounts of millet, corn, buckwheat, and rye are okay as long as constipation is not present.
- Asparagus, beets, carrots, daikon, green beans, cooked dark leafy greens, peas, celery, summer squashes, winter squashes, sweet potatoes, yams are the best vegetables. In smaller amounts, eat broccoli, cauliflower, and cabbage.
- Cook vegetables in ghee or oils such as sesame, almond, olive, or sunflower with added water.
- Cook with mild spices such as asafoetida, cardamom, cumin, coriander, ginger, fennel, dill, cinnamon, mustard seed, and black pepper. Nuts and seeds in small amounts will work, particularly if soaked. Split mung beans, adzuki beans, tofu, and small amounts of brown lentils are the best legumes.
- Any of the seaweeds are excellent in cooked dishes.
- Fresh fruits to favor include apricots, avocado, ripe bananas, berries, cherries, coconut, dates, limes, fresh figs, peaches, plums, mangoes, pineapple, papayas, and tamarind. Soak or cook raisins and prunes. Cook apples and pears before eating.
- Ghee, cottage cheese, fresh buttermilk, and raw or unhomogenized milk are best in moderate amounts.

- The best sweeteners are juices, maple syrup, dates, and Sucanat. Avoid raw apples, pomegranates, and dried fruit. Cooked apples are fine.

Daily routine is critical to balancing vata.
- Increase warm herbal teas, stillness, relaxation, meditation, calm Yoga asana (postures), and validation of self.
- Decrease rushing, hurrying, cold, dryness, fear, cold salads, and very hot spices.

PITTA FOODS

Foods that are cooling, liquid, and refreshing are best for balancing the pitta dosha.

- Grains such as oats, barley, cracked wheat, spelt, basmati rice (brown and white), sweet brown rice, and sushi rice are best.
- Vegetables include kales, collards, lettuces, asparagus, green beans, artichokes, cucumbers, celery, broccoli, cauliflower, cabbage, parsnip, peas, sweet potatoes, yams, squashes, pumpkin, and sprouts.
- The best spices are coriander, dill, cardamom, cilantro, curry leaves, fresh basil, fennel, turmeric, ginger, and saffron. Occasionally, cinnamon, nutmeg, or a bit of black pepper is okay.
- Use ghee, flax, olive, sunflower, and coconut oils.
- Almonds soaked and peeled, roasted sunflower, or pumpkin seeds and coconuts are the best nuts for the pitta dosha.
- The best beans and legumes are split mung beans, split peas, adzuki beans, tofu, lima beans, garbanzo beans, and black beans.
- Seaweeds in moderate amounts are okay.

- Fresh seasonal fruits such as apples, apricots, berries, cherries, coconuts, dates, fresh figs, grapes, pears, tangerines, mangoes, pineapples, plums, kiwi, limes, and sweet oranges.
- Ghee, cottage cheese, warmed cow milk with cooling spices, and fresh yogurt in moderate amounts is okay.
- The best sweeteners are fruit juices, agave nectar, barley malt, maple syrup, dates, and Sucanat.
- Avoid chocolate, honey, molasses, cheese, yogurt, onions, garlic, radishes, raw spinach, and any sour, salty, spicy, or pungent foods. Minimize spices such as asafoetida, dry ginger, fenugreek, salt, and mustard seed.
- Minimize sour fruits such as grapefruits, lemons, olives, and papayas.
- Decrease sour, pungent, and salty foods (pickles, fermented foods, chilies, etc.).

Calm pitta dosha with cooling, calming foods and activities.

- Cooling drinks such as aloe vera juice and rose water, calming massage with coconut oil, noncompetitive Yoga asana (postures) and devotional meditation.
- Minimize competitive, aggressive, and hot environments.

KAPHA FOODS

Foods that are warm, stimulating, light, and with less oils and fats balance the kapha dosha.

- Grains such as barley, buckwheat, millet, quinoa, rye, and corn in cereal, cracked or whole grain are best. Basmati rice (brown and white), quinoa, and amaranth are okay occasionally. Minimize wheat, rice, and oats as they are mucous forming.
- The best vegetables are kales, collards, bok choy, turnips (root and green), lettuces, arugula, asparagus, green beans, artichokes, beets, broccoli, carrots, celery, corn, jicama, ginger, cauliflower, brussel sprouts, cabbage, parsnips, peas, radishes, sprouts, summer squashes, spinach, and pumpkin.
- Cook with spices such as cinnamon, cloves, rosemary, coriander, mustard seeds, saffron, cumin, basil, curry leaves, nutmeg, bay leaf, black pepper, dill, thyme, caraway, oregano, turmeric cardamom, ginger, cayenne, parsley, cilantro, spearmint, and peppermint for the best balance.
- Moderate to smaller amounts of oils such as flax or sunflower oils and ghee. Roasted sunflower or pumpkin seeds are okay, but minimize any other nuts.
- Adzuki, whole or split mung, soy, lima, black, and garbanzos are the best beans. Split peas, red lentils, and tofu are also good for kapha dosha.
- Kombu is good for cooking legumes and small amounts of other seaweeds work well in sautés and salads.
- Fruits best for kapha dosha are apples, pears, apricots, berries, cherries, peaches, pomegranates, and raisins. Occasional tangerines, mangoes, and limes are okay.

- Small amounts of ghee, goat's milk, unsalted goat cheese, or raw cow milk watered down fifty-fifty with spices are best to minimize mucous formation.
- A pinch of fresh ginger with a few drops of lemon juice before each meal will aid digestion.
- Minimize sweeteners using only a small amount of honey in herbal tea to reduce mucous.
- Avoid salt, nuts, chocolate, whole milk, cheese, and yogurt.
- Reduce oils and any other heavy, oily, or cold food.
- Eat before sunset.
- Avoid snacks and overeating in one sitting.
- Reduce cold, dampness, wet foods, and sweet, sour, and salty tastes as in yogurt, sugar, and salt.

Keep kapha moving for best results.

- Increase exercise such as vinyasa Yoga asana (flowing postures), deep massage, saunas, drinks of warm water and spicy herbal teas.
- Also, increase opportunities for letting go, giving, and sharing.

ADDING NEW FOODS TO YOUR DIET

Add new foods into your daily life gradually. If you are the rebellious type, changing too quickly can cause a setback. Pause, go inside, and find your truth. Ask yourself "What commitment am I willing to make?" Listen to the answer, whether you like it or not. Go with what you can commit to and explore the feelings about why you are not willing to commit to things you would like to do that are in your best interest.

When introduced to Ayurvedic cooking, people have a tendency to think it's "just Indian food." This is not correct. Ayurvedic cooking is not just Indian food, and all Indian food is definitely not Ayurvedic in content or preparation.

One of the ancient texts of Ayurveda, the Charaka Samhita, says, "One should not select food articles based on habit or ignorance. After examination, use only wholesome foods, as one's formation precisely reflects the food consumed." Be aware of the tendency to pick one or two foods and eat them all of the time out of habit. Some variation is important for nutritional content and satisfying the palate. Do not wait until you are "bored" with a food. This is a sign of habitual eating. Choose food with discrimination and moderate your intake. Let your new ways evolve as you change and grow.

Food, and how you consume it, is an avenue for nurturing yourself and others. Food can bring unity and spirituality to your life when consumed with a clear, positive sacred attitude. Clearing unconsciousness to allow in the new is an essential part of the healing process. By bringing consciousness into your relationship with food and eating, you can provide healthy nurturing for yourself and others.

Working with the freshest possible food, you can rediscover your place in nature. Acknowledge the plants, animals, people, earth, sun, water, and other things that contribute to your food and mealtime. It will improve your well-being and that of those around you.

Utilizing practices to move toward physical and mental purity cultivates connection to your innermost self. You will find compassion, sweetness, acceptance, patience, and tolerance. How you eat is just as important as what you eat. A simple meal filled with prana and love makes it easy to see that all is well in the world right in this very moment. Your attitude while eating and shortly after eating is as important as the food itself.

There are so many types of foods and beverages available today. It can be confusing to choose among them. Foods from your locale and the current season are two significant factors to look for. Selecting foods according to your individual constitution, your current state of balance or imbalance and the condition of your agni are the most important considerations. If these are new considerations for you, incorporate them gradually. Based on the information provided in this book, establish a list of the balancing foods and drinks to focus on for yourself and your family members. It will become much easier over time. Do not expect to do it all at once.

RETHINKING HOW YOU SHOP

Shopping for food can be a daunting task for many people. You may not have been exposed to this growing up. It can be enjoyable! Shopping for food is a valuable part of your self-nurturing. Notice your attitude right now, toward reading this. What are you saying to yourself? Are you attached to your view of yourself and the idea "this is how I am"? The ego hangs on to the idea of being right. It will sacrifice anything just to be right—even changes that make sense.

Release your resistance now, to the entire process of acquiring food and drink. Release resistance to their meaning and importance in your life. Cup your hands together out in front of you and put the resistance into your hands. Now open your hands and *let go*.

Answer the following questions for yourself:

- Do you buy things such as food, clothing or anything to avoid feelings?
- Do you go shopping for other things and not shop for good food when you want to avoid or stuff feelings?
- Are you unwilling to buy good food for yourself because it costs a little more or requires some effort to find?
- Do you only buy certain brand names of food because they are familiar to you, regardless of the content?
- Do you put more effort into taking care of your car or your appliances than your own well-being through eating?

Consider these very important points to assist you in going beyond mainstream programming:

- Make a commitment to yourself and your family to consume only fresh, healthy, unprocessed, cleanly grown food. The rewards will show on many levels for you, your family, and the planet.
- Make a list of your intended purchases for a guide while shopping, but also be open to what is fresh that day.
- Just because you do not see, taste, or smell things like pesticides, herbicides, chemical fertilizers, hormones, and antibiotics in your food does not mean they are not there. They are in our water supplies as well as food. They are likely having a negative effect on your health and well-being.
- Purchasing cheap commercial food to save a couple of dollars leads to spending large amounts of money on drugs and doctors to fix the problems caused by the poor-quality food. Spend a few dollars more to buy better-quality food.

- Do not believe everything you read. Ask questions, explore, and be aware of your own experience.

There are simple tools you can use to help raise your consciousness while shopping. Before shopping, clear your energy by grounding and connecting to the earth and to your source. Here is a method for doing that:

Pause. Find the center of your head by imagining a line between the eyebrows and straight back and from the tops of the ears straight across. Where the two lines cross is the center of your head. Place your attention in the center of your head. Imagine an energetic cord, as large as you like, going from the base of your spine down to the center of the planet. Imagine hooking it in and turning it on "release." Let go of anything that is not you. Let go of "shoulds," "supposed to," and any voices or considerations that are not your own. Feel yourself grounded and letting go of anything that is not you. Allow the planet to strengthen you and help you find your center and truth in this moment. This takes a matter of seconds, with eyes open or closed. You can stand, sit, or lie down. Next, be aware of the energetic bubble, or aura, around your body. See it as whole and clear of anything that is not you. Then, enjoy a sense of clarity as you do your food shopping.

Go to the market two or more times each week. Allow it to be an important and enjoyable part of your life. If you ask a family member to go shopping, be sure the list is clear so that you will end up with what you had intended. Encourage an attitude of enthusiasm. Shopping as a family when you are making changes can sometimes be very helpful. Employ an experienced guide to help you and take a list of new choices to explore. Go shopping when you are feeling centered and collected—not when you are hungry, emotional, or tired. If you feel this way all of the time, see if you are living according to your priorities. Perhaps you need to start saying no to some things or delegate some of your activities and get more sleep.

Note the hours of operation of your favorite health food store or local farmer's market and make a point of shaping your schedule accordingly. You are worth it. Develop relationships with the produce manager and attendants. Find out as much as possible about the sources of the food and be grateful for their work. They are handling your food.

Let the shopping experience be an adventure. Visit a local farm and get to know them. Learn about what and how they grow. Bring children when they are ready to participate. Seeing where their food is grown is a great opportunity for children.

Purchase only foods that are high in prana. If food does not exude prana, do not buy it. Buy local fresh produce whenever possible. It will be in season and most balancing for your system, assuming the particular item is appropriate for your doshas. As you choose food that increases your energetic frequency, you contribute to raising consciousness on the planet.

Prana is not only life force but consciousness, as well. A simple exercise to learn to recognize prana in your food involves pausing in your life for a few moments. Close the eyes and go inside to that neutral point in the center of your head, just above the pineal gland. Imagining the center of your head is enough. You need no visualization. See a thread of white energy connecting that point in the center of your head with your crown at the top of your head. Next, imagine the very sweet point at the center of your chest in your heart center. Connect these two points with a thread of light. Breathe deeply and slowly for five breaths. Then open your eyes, rub the palms of your hands together a few times to wake them up, and feel your energy in them. If you do not feel anything then imagining is enough.

If this is new to you, take your hands out to the sides and very slowly bring the palms toward each other. Go slowly. You will feel a sensation—that is your energy. It may feel solid, light, warm, cool, tingly, or many other possibilities. All are okay. Now that your senses are awake, move your palm slowly toward a food item and notice what you feel. It may be subtle, very strong, or nothing. Move slowly and keep your attention in the center point in your head. Compare some items to feel the differences. Speak aloud about what you feel. It is okay; it will help to validate your experience. If your head is chattering about how silly this is, laugh at yourself and keep going anyway.

Practice feeling prana at home with a couple of fresh food items and an inert object such as an empty plastic bag. Feel the difference.

If you feel nothing over an item, it has no prana. Choose something else to eat that has prana. Food without prana turns into ama that accumulates in your body systems as metabolic waste, eventually resulting in disease.

Feeling the prana is a great exercise for children and adults. You can use it with all the food and beverage that you consume. Note how you feel after eating food with prana versus food without it. Eating and drinking food with prana will give you greater vitality and improved health, so make your food choices accordingly.

Buy locally to support your local farmers and your community. The farmers' job is challenging. Support farming practices that are healthy for humans, animals, and the earth. It may require some investigation and education to find the best way to do this.

Do not assume all items in the health food store are good for you. Additionally, do not assume because it says "organic" or "natural" that it is good to consume. Many of these items are heavily processed and have little to no prana. Learn what the various methods of growing food are, such as organic, unsprayed, biodynamic, noncommercial, and commercial. It can vary somewhat according to your marketplace. The government standards have allowed the use of many questionable items in the classification of "organically grown." Do your research and make a conscious choice when you buy.

Local farmers' markets and produce stands are often very good, assuming the food is actually local. If the source is not obvious, ask questions about where and how the items were grown. If they cannot answer your questions, you may want to move to the next stand. In addition to obtaining fresh food, the interactions with farmers will benefit you and the farmer greatly in terms of health and harmony.

Fruits and vegetables that do not look picture perfect can still contain prana. Realize that a small flaw in the skin of a fruit or vegetable has little to do with what it has to offer you in terms of taste and nourishment. I remember in the 1960s when my grandfather could not sell an entire season of watermelons to the large food stores because they had small marks on the outside of the skin. The insides were perfect and beautiful. No disease was present.

In all cases, feel the prana. If food has no prana, it will not benefit your body, mind, or spirit—regardless of its appearance or growing methods. If it has been sitting on a truck, in a warehouse or your refrigerator for too long, there will be little if any prana. Choose food that has prana.

Find ways to trade fruits or vegetables with your neighbors. If your fruit trees provide more than you can consume, call in a friend to help distribute the ripe fruit. Do not let it go to waste. Start a trading group among your neighbors. Give any excess to a food bank or agency that can use it to help others. It only takes a small amount of time to find a grateful recipient of the food.

Use as little packaged foods as possible. Most of it has little if any prana, becomes ama in your system, and adds to the trash going into the landfill. If you choose to purchase packaged foods, read the entire ingredients list. If you cannot understand what is on the list, do not eat it. Preservatives are harmful to ingest. When looking at the nutritional information, recognize that the nutritional content typically is measured before processing. Very little of the listed nutrients are actually available or assimilated by your body. You will be healthier, spend less money, and put less into the landfill by choosing fresh, unprocessed food.

Make your visit to the store or market an adventure into new creative possibilities.

Your Kitchen and Dining Area

Honor and respect the kitchen and dining areas as sacred spaces. What does this mean? Bring in your very best attitude and highest sense of being. Pause before you begin and consciously acknowledge what you are about to do—prepare nourishing food with love and gratitude. Keep other activities out of this area. In particular, take any negativity or intense discussions elsewhere. Do your best to use the kitchen and dining are only for preparing and eating food and not for business, television, movies, or other extroverted activities.

If you are designing or building a house, place the kitchen in a corner or separate area that enhances the collection of sacred energy. The southeast corner is ideal. Do not designate the kitchen as a throughway. If possible, plant an herb or vegetable garden in view of the kitchen. Looking outside at herbs or vegetables you can use in your meal is a sweet reminder of where the ingredients come from and how you are part of nature. If your home is small with an open floor plan exposing the kitchen, cover the TV, computer, or other electronic equipment with a decorative cloth. This simple act will help keep other energy separate from preparing food and eating. In addition, adequate ventilation and natural lighting is important.

Eliminate clutter from the kitchen and dining areas. Keeping the space clean, inviting, and comfortable provides the best opportunity for optimal digestion and enjoyment of the meal. Set the energy of the space for nurturing, nourishment, peace, freedom, and love. Decorate these rooms with soothing and inviting art and furniture. Recognize that something special is happening here, and it will. Allow the space to support you in your unity with self and others with whom you prepare the food and dine.

Attend to your storage needs with the same care. Maintain easy access to your food items and cooking utensils. Make it easy to find what you need. Get rid of utensils you are not using. Use glass storage jars when possible for herbs, spices and other foods and label them in case you forget what they are. Organization in the kitchen will keep your cooking process smooth—your intuition and creative energy will flow more easily. Remember, if you are angry about not being able to find ingredients, that energy will find its way into your food. Keep dried spices six months or less and store them in a dark storage container or cupboard. Throw out old spices and foods in your cupboards and refrigerator.

Be selective about your appliances. When you are preparing food for one or two people, manual tools rather than electric may be sufficient. Working with your hands adds your energy to the food. Keep the electric gadgets to a minimum.

The quality of the cookware you use is important. Stay away from aluminum and nonstick finishes. They both leach substances that are damaging to humans and the environment. Good quality stainless steel, copper, cast iron, or glass cookware work well. There are some very nice, reasonably priced, handmade clay cooking pots and dishes available today with nontoxic, natural glazes. A natural clay pot has the loving energy of the person who made it, which adds wonderfully to your food preparation.

A good-quality stainless steel pressure cooker is a helpful tool for preparing grains, beans, and legumes in particular. It reduces or eliminates the need for soaking and reduces the preparation time significantly. I resisted using a pressure cooker for many years as I had a samskara about the lid blowing off as a child. I even bought one and gave it away without using it. Realizing the extent of my samskara and witnessing the ease and safety of using a pressure cooker helped me heal and move on. They are now quite secure and safe when used properly.

Keep a sharp set of knives so that foods are easy to cut and prepare. Efficient tools make the preparation process fun instead of a burden. There are easy-to-use sharpening stones available. Electric knife sharpeners are also available at a reasonable price.

The positive energy you put into your cooking collects on your cookware and utensils, contributing to the welfare of you and your family. Use your cookware only for cooking foods and drinks, not for craft projects or with other substances. Keep your food preparation tools in the kitchen and your loving energy will collect on them. If you think the notion of good energy collecting on the cookware and utensils is silly, try an experiment at your next meal. Send loving energy consciously to the cookware and food without telling anyone. Notice what happens when you serve the meal. Notice the comments others make to you and how you feel during and after eating. See for yourself. You may find you would like to use your own special plate, bowl, and utensils. Try this and see if you notice a difference.

Remove or avoid using the microwave oven. Microwave ovens destroy the prana in food. They interfere with your energy when you are close to them during operation. Consider getting rid of your microwave oven. Move it outside first. Observe how much better you feel. Your food preparation time may require more awareness at first. The benefits will quickly outweigh any perceived challenges.

A friend once convinced me to try heating water in a microwave. The difference was outstanding. The water tasted flat and lifeless. An interesting report of a children's science project addresses the use of microwave ovens. They watered two plants of the same size and type, one with tap water and the other with water heated in a microwave and let cool. In just three days, the plant receiving the microwave water was drooping, and the other plant was thriving. If this is not enough to convince you, try it for yourself. Work with your own evidence rather than waiting until someone tells you in the newspaper or on the radio about a health hazard. Are you feeding yourself lifeless matter called food?

THE BASICS OF PREPARING FOOD

Food preparation is a form of expression. Give of yourself purposefully and move creatively through it rather than doing it in drudgery. Replenish yourself with trust, acceptance, creativity, peace, joy, and freedom. Clear your energy, ground yourself, and align yourself with nature as suggested in the Meditation for clearing your energy later in this book. In particular, release fear, anger, and unconsciousness prior to preparing a meal.

If you are not able to let go of anger and negativity, ask someone else who is clear to prepare the food. If this is not possible, wait to prepare the food until you are clear. Your energy will clear when you surrender your negative focus and attachment. Connect yourself to a higher plane of creativity and consciousness just by imagining that connection. If you feel like you do not know how, stop what you are doing. Close your eyes if possible. Imagine yourself taking a step up the next stair of a staircase. As you take this step, allow yourself to feel the sensation in your body. It may be tingling, warmth, coolness, or some other sensation. First, move one foot and then the other. Just by taking your mind through this exercise, you will begin to raise your own vibration.

Transcend your thinking and limited beliefs. Go beyond your current boundaries. Harmonize with nature and the higher vibrations of the universe. Realize you are a part of the Divine reality. Be in this place. Even a moment will stimulate a shift in your attitude and energy. Giggle at yourself.

Your attitude and energy go into the food and then into those who eat it. Your hands and five fingers relate directly to the five elements. These same five elements are in the food you are preparing. The combination of the elements is what is sacred in the food. Either the food you prepare will contribute to well-being, or it will contribute to lowering the vibration of those who partake in it. This lower vibration detracts from health and harmony.

Once you clear your energy, you can work creatively. If food preparation is new for you or you are moving away from old ways, realize that change is a process. Let it be a sensual experience: see, feel, smell, and hear the food in its preparation. Be present in the process. As with any new activity, some meals will be more successful than others will. Learn from each adventure and carry the learning forward to the next time. A verse from the Upanishads says it very well:

May the Universe never abuse food.
Breath is food.
The body eats food.
The body rests on breath.
Breath rests on the body.
Food is resting on food.
The one who knows this becomes rich in food and great in spirit.
—Taittiriya Upanishad 11.7

Keep the preparation very simple. Two to four prana-filled foods are plenty and make a fulfilling meal. Take notes in this book or make note cards as tools. Remember that recipes are great tools but are not carved in stone. Many variations are possible; the more you play with them, the more interesting the results will be. Eventually, with practice and letting go, you will be able to look at the food you have available and come up with an interesting, balanced meal. For those days when you do not feel creative, this book can remind you of the possibilities.

For example, if you are baking muffins, check the recipe first then your cupboards to see which ingredients you have and what substitutions you can use. Often you do not need everything called for in the recipe. The result can still be lovely. Many different grains are good alternatives for baking flour. Some possibilities include the following: nuts, raisins or another dried fruit, or fresh fruit. The most important thing is to learn the essence of the recipe or the type of food you are preparing. Step beyond your typical thinking, be flexible, and explore. There are many yummy possibilities!

The method used to prepare foods affects the doshas and your body. There are a number of common cooking techniques, and each of them results in qualities in the food that offer you different opportunities for balance and harmony. Appendix E consists of a list of cooking techniques and the qualities they impart to the food. Although the techniques are common, giving some thought to the effects they create in your body can assist you in planning meals that are balancing. For example, if you are feeling cold and dry, likely too much vata, foods that are blended, baked, and soaked would be balancing and reduce vata. If you are exhausted or about to get sick, eating soups that are lightly boiled will be easy to digest and will be easier for agni. If you are feeling heavy and lethargic, eat lighter foods such as steamed vegetables with sprouts. Cook with the quality that is opposite the imbalance you feel.

Remember, like increases like, and the opposite brings balance to your current state. Always look at what it takes to come back to balance and harmony. The doshas are dynamic and changing in response to everything on the inside and outside of you. Change of season, lifestyle, and stages of life all require adjustments to maintain the dosha balance.

Relate what you did in the preparation to the results in your food. You satisfy the palate, the eye, and the sense of self when you are creative, light, loving, and accepting in your attitude while preparing food. Is there anything better to do than offer up your love and appreciation in food and drink for yourself and for others?

When you habituate being sad, angry, depressed, or discontented, you forget that you possess choices. When you feel like you do not have a choice, act as if you do. Do what you would do with that choice. Your perspective can change quickly if you become willing, let go, and allow your attitude to shift. Then laugh at yourself.

When the food you are preparing has prana, you will feel the positive effect if you remain aware during the food preparation and eating. It takes practice and a little time. Make friends with food and drink. Let them connect you to the whole of life and nature.

Notice how you feel when you participate in the richness of preparing your own food. Acknowledge who grew the food, who brought it to you, and realize your connection to everything. You will feel better after eating and increase your overall well-being. It takes only a small amount of time.

Involve friends and family in your food preparation. Making food together brings connection and helps everyone grow in his or her connection to the sacred. Notice if you want everything to be perfect. See where you can let go and allow someone else to be a part of the process. Focus on love and appreciation as you prepare the food and let go of perfectionism. Sincere appreciation makes a difference on all levels.

I refer to the types of food I work with in this book. If you eat animal flesh, similar principles apply concerning attitude, cleanliness, and preparation.

Clean up as you walk through food preparation and immediately after a meal. Cleaning is the same as preparing: a cheerful, selfless attitude brings harmony to the kitchen and the food. Do not leave dirty dishes in the sink. Leaving dirty dishes and food lying around in the kitchen is similar to leaving clutter in your head. Clear it out so that nothing collects there.

As you practice consciously preparing your own food, it will become easier to prepare the optimal amounts. The prana in the food goes down after cooking and sitting. Leftovers have little to no prana.

If you make too much food at a meal, offer it to someone in need, to friends or family. Offer it while fresh, rather than letting it sit in the refrigerator to get old or go bad. If you do eat leftovers, do so within 8 hours of preparation. Let them come to room temperature for eating or add some warm water. Reheating will destroy any remaining prana. Notice how you feel after eating leftovers compared to a freshly prepared meal. Make a conscious choice to eat prana-filled fresh food and your health and vitality will improve.

Keep certain basic foods in your kitchen at all times. Include whole grains, legumes, ghee, oils, spices, fresh and dried herbs, natural sweeteners, nuts, dried fruits, fresh fruits, and fresh vegetables on this list. Be aware of the list of sattvic foods in this book as a starting point. Then select those foods that will help balance your constitution. You may find yourself working with new types of foods. The following information will help to acquaint you with these foods.

Eat **whole grains** rather than refined grains such as pastas or couscous. Examples are steel cut oats, pearl barley, millet, oat groats, buckwheat groats, bulgar wheat, amaranth, teff, quinoa, brown and white basmati rice, wild rice, and others. Many people shy away from making whole grains because of the length of time required to cook them. If you soak grains the night before or a few hours before cooking, the cooking time reduces to less than half. Rinse grains with pure clean water using your clean hands to move the grains until the water runs clear. Some grains, such as quinoa, have a powder coating that is very difficult to digest. Use the soaking water for cooking the grains. You may also use herbal or medicinal teas for cooking grain, adding flavor and the qualities of the tea.

For **beans** and **legumes**, consider using split mung beans (whole mung beans with the hull removed and split), whole mung beans, adzuki beans, garbanzo beans (chick peas), split peas, red lentils, urid dhal (black lentils that are white without the shell), brown lentils, and other local beans available. Fresh beans are preferable when available. A few simple techniques make them easy to prepare and digest. Soak beans four to eight hours (overnight) prior to cooking. Throw out the soak water or put it in your compost if you have it. Cooking beans with asafoetida makes the beans easier to digest and adds flavor. Including sea vegetables such as kombu or wakame adds the salty taste and trace minerals. Bring the beans to a boil then turn them to simmer. Place a lid on the pot leaving a small opening for the gases to escape. Beans and legumes cook much more quickly and easily in a pressure cooker. See halepule. com for information and tips on using a pressure cooker.

Split mung and **lentils** respond well to light roasting to bring out the flavor. Place in a pan with ghee or oil and stir for a few minutes over heat. Add the spices and continue to stir until the aroma is noticeable; after only a minute or two add warm water to the pot. Use warm water rather than cold to bring out the flavor. Urid dhal and chana dhal are both rich in vitality but heavy on their own. They are best in combination with split mung beans, split peas, or one of the lentils.

Sea vegetables are a good source of vitamins, chlorophyll, enzymes, dietary fiber, and natural salts. Sea vegetables provide a rich source of nutrients that are easily digestible. There are a variety of types including kombu, sea palm, nori, hiziki, and arame—each with varying characteristics. Look for sun-dried, wild crafted, and sustainably harvested sea vegetables rather than artificially dried and farmed. Choose a brand that is from the ocean closest to where you live.

Next are the **oils** to cook with and add to your food. **Ghee** is a very special item that you can make yourself from organic, unsalted butter or purchase already prepared. Ghee is butter that has been cooked until its biochemistry changes, rendering it more extractive in quality than butter and supportive of agni and dosha balance. Butter is congestive in your system while ghee draws out toxins. Use it for cooking or as a condiment. It stimulates agni, improves digestion, and is used medicinally both orally and on the body in Ayurveda.

You may find ghee in the refrigerated section of stores as required by law, but refrigerating the ghee reduces its beneficial qualities. Keep ghee at room temperature in the cupboard. Be careful not to contaminate it with a used or wet utensil. Mold will grow on contaminated ghee while properly stored ghee improves with age. Find instructions for making ghee in Appendix A and at halepule.com.

Oils such as sesame, sunflower, olive, almond, coconut, avocado, macadamia nut, and others are beneficial when used in moderation. Keep the oils in a cool, dark place and always check the smell for freshness before using. Rancid oil is toxic for humans and animals. Use rancid oil to fuel diesel engines, not your body. Cooking at high temperatures breaks down the oils causing problems for those who eat them. Avoid these problems by cooking at moderate and low temperatures. Cook with moderate heat and your food will retain more prana, taste better, and digest more easily, resulting in higher nutrient absorption.

Select the best oils to work with according to your constitution. Your body most easily assimilates unrefined cold-pressed oils. Sauté your spices in oil until the aroma comes up first to wake up the prana and then stir in the vegetables and simmer together with a desired amount of water. The vegetables will gently steam along with the sautéing. This approach is helpful for keeping all doshas in balance.

I suggest staying away from processed oils where the contents are not clearly stated. Avoid products with labels such as "vegetable oil" or "cooking oil" for example. The precise ingredients are unknown and likely from an inferior source. This is an area to raise your consciousness. If the company supplying it was happy with or even knew the ingredients, they would list them. Inferior products are cheaper because they are inferior. By consuming low-quality products, you will pay a price in how you feel and in your well-being.

Spices and herbs are not so mysterious. They are a beneficial addition to food when used appropriately. In moderate amounts and correct combinations according to their attributes, they are excellent for balancing the system, aiding in digestion, and enhancing the taste of food. When used in excess, they can disturb the digestion and contribute to over activity of the mind.

You can grow fresh herbs for yourself in pots or purchase them at the farmers' market or store. Store them in glass containers with a sprinkle of water in the refrigerator. Most will last longer this way. All of the herbs and spices can balance tastes and qualities in a meal such as adding heat to your system, cooling your system, and aiding in digestion.

The spice guide below is an easy beginner reference to help you optimize the use of herbs and spices. Try one or two at a time if they are new for you. If you are accustomed to processed foods that contain large amounts of sugar, caffeine, salt, and other chemicals, use spices such as cumin, coriander, fresh ginger, and turmeric to aid your transition.

Select the spices you want to use and cook them in the order on this list. Notice that the hard seeds come first so that the longer cooking will bring out their taste. Add the fresh herbs toward the end. You can also hand grind the seeds before cooking to bring out their flavor.

coriander seed
"sweet" spices:
    cardamom pods
    cinnamon sticks
    whole peppercorns
    cloves
black mustard seed
cumin seed
nuts:
    almonds
    cashews
    hazelnuts
    pecans
aromatics:
    fenugreek
    curry leaves
    asafoetida
    fennel seeds
    bay leaves
fresh curry leaves
sesame seeds
fresh coconut
dry coconut
turmeric (fresh, powder)
ginger (fresh, powder)
fresh chilies*
fresh garlic*
fresh onion*

The following spices are aids in digestion. You may find them fresh, in dried seeds, and powdered. Fresh spices are ideal, although most forms are good. Certain spices change qualities when they are powdered. Ginger, for instance, is more heating and drying when in powder form. Store spices in a cool dark place for best retention of prana. Light breaks down the prana.

asafoetida (hing)
- dispels gas and cramping; good for cooking beans and legumes, as well as vegetables.
- destroys parasites, cleanses intestinal tract

bay leaf
- warming, digestive aid

black mustard seeds
- digestive aid
- dispels gas and toxins
- stimulates circulation
- reduces vata

black pepper
- increases pitta; pacifies vata and kapha
- destroys digestive toxins
- antidote for excessive raw foods

cardamom
- stimulates agni
- pacifies all doshas
- increases joy and vitality in the body
- neutralizes mucus-formation from milk

cinnamon
- pacifies vata and kapha
- strengthens and harmonizes the circulation, heart, and kidneys
- digestive, warming

cloves
- heating, digestive aid

coriander seed
- cooling, dispels gas and bloating, digestive
- pacifies all doshas
- excellent for the urinary tract

cumin
- dispels gas, digestive aid
- antidote for pungent foods
- pacifies vata and kapha, balancing for all doshas in moderation

fennel
- cooling, digestive

fenugreek
- warming, digestive
- pacifies vata and kapha
- rejuvenates and tones the entire body

garlic*
- warming, reduces ama in small amounts
- increases pitta; pacifies vata and kapha
- natural antibiotic
- in excess dulls and irritates the mind

ginger
- pacifies vata and kapha
- relieves gas, cramps, and nausea
- stimulates agni
- digests toxins in the body

saffron
- balances all doshas, digestive, cooling
- regulates menstrual cycle
- increases love, devotion, and compassion

turmeric
- balances all doshas, heating
- purifies blood, mind, and skin
- anti-inflammatory in moderate amounts
- cleanses chakras, subtle channels, and restores ligaments
- helps digest protein
- promotes balanced metabolism

kombu
- digestive, removes heavy metals

lemon
- increases pitta

lime
- balancing to all doshas

onion**
- strengthening
- increases appetite

*Increases rajas (minimize if you prefer a harmonious mind)
**Some say rajas and some say tamas (minimize if you prefer a harmonious mind)

Dairy consumption has developed a bad reputation in our culture. From an Ayurvedic perspective, consuming dairy in as pure a state as possible is best. This means without added hormones, antibiotics, preservatives, and residuals of herbicides and pesticides. It also means at room temperature or warm. Ideally, cows or goats would be grazed free range and treated humanely. Dairy is a beautiful, nurturing gift from the animal and has those qualities in its essence. My experience is that the more sweetly the animals are treated, the better tasting the milk. If given the opportunity to try fresh raw milk from a goat or cow, you will see the enormous difference from processed milk.

The contamination and processing of dairy products contribute significantly to the allergies that many people develop to these foods. Other significant factors contributing to problems with dairy are eating too large a quantity and consuming it at cold temperatures. Dairy is heavy and difficult to digest when cold and in large quantities. Consume dairy products warm or at room temperature in very small quantities with as little processing as possible. For example, half a cup or less of fresh yogurt or buttermilk cut in half with warm water and spices at the end of a meal is an aid to digestion. A large glass of cold milk with a meal or a bowl of cold commercial yogurt is heavy, harmful to digestion, and turns to ama in your system.

Condiments are something to consume in small amounts, if at all. If the food is not good enough on its own, would you be better off not eating it? Ask yourself, "Does this food have prana to offer, and is eating it in my best interest?" If not, pouring on another tamasic substance, such as commercial ketchup, will only create more ama in your system. It may satisfy your short-term craving, but notice the price of not feeling great afterward. Going unconscious around food takes you down the old path. Choose the new path, raising your own vibration.

Fresh condiments in small quantities can contribute to balance and well-being. Many commercially made condiments have a reasonable list of ingredients—meaning they are without added salt, sugar, and chemical preservatives. Yet, prana is almost nonexistent in them. Real benefit can come from fresh condiments.

Making your own chutneys and sauces with fresh ingredients to enhance digestion as well as flavor is rewarding. They are very easy to prepare in a blender or a small pot. There are examples in Appendix A.

Flax meal is a nice addition to a soup, salad, or grain. It has many valuable nutrients and adds a pleasant flavor. Buy flax seeds in bulk. Grind them in a blender as you eat them, or grind small amounts and keep them in a closed glass container in the refrigerator. The flax meal will lose its prana if left out in the air. Whole flax seed is not digestible.

Natural sweeteners may be useful in certain preparations. Some choices are pure maple syrup, agave nectar, rice syrup, barley malt, Sucanat, and honey. Lovely alternatives for dessert preparations are apple juice, carrot juice, and soaked raisins or other dried fruit with the juice. Remember, if you are preparing food with prana, you may not need to add sweetener—even if a recipe calls for it.

Honey is considered the nectar of the gods. It is heating in quality, so consume it in small quantities. Do not cook or boil honey as it becomes toxic in your system. It turns into a glue like substance that adheres to mucous membranes, clogs the *nadis* (subtle energy channels), and produces ama. Stir it into warm drinks and put it on warm foods. Maple syrup is cooling in its effect and better for anyone with too much heat or imbalanced pitta. Stevia, although from a natural source is very potent. Although said to be okay for diabetics to process, it is a challenge for the body-mind connection and seems to promote attachment and craving for many people. All synthetic sweeteners are tamas, without prana, and best avoided.

People getting off refined sugar should minimize sweeteners of any sort. Unrefined natural sugar is sometimes part of Ayurvedic herbal preparations as a carrier for the herbs. The amounts are small and balanced with the other items in the preparation.

Eating heavily processed foods and refined sugar numbs your taste buds. They become dull to the subtle natural tastes causing the tongue to look for stronger sugary and heavy food. It takes time to clear the taste buds and for the senses to regain their sensitivity and clarity.

The body, mind, and spirit connection of a human is highly sensitive. When you are working to bring this connection back to its natural state of harmony, it is best to stay away from concentrated forms of sweeteners. Keep what you consume as close to its natural state as possible. If you are not sure, ask someone who has experience in this area. Be aware and responsible for your choices.

Nuts in small amounts can be a beneficial addition to your eating plan. Hazelnuts, almonds, pecans, macadamia, cashews, pistachios, pine nuts and walnuts are all possibilities. Nuts, like any other food, are best when lightly cooked or soaked. Small amounts, such as one handful cooked in your meal, can be agreeable; large amounts will cause digestive disturbance and aggravate pitta. If eaten in excess, they can cause imbalance in the lining of the intestines resulting in gas, overgrowth of yeast, and ama. Peanuts are not included in this list because they are difficult to digest and assimilate and cause a significant allergic reaction in some people. Best to avoid them.

Nuts stored for extended periods grow mold in them that is not always obvious to the consumer. Consuming moldy nuts promotes imbalance in the intestines, allergies, and ama. The nut is not necessarily the problem, the mold is.

Cashews are not actually a nut, but the fruit of the tree. They are best when cooked in small quantities and are toxic when raw or in large quantities.

Soak almonds overnight and peel them for best eating. The skin contains tannic acid, which disturbs digestion. If they agree with you, try eating twelve peeled almonds each morning with your breakfast and see how you feel.

Seeds such as sunflower, sesame, pumpkin, and hemp may also provide nutrients and a tasty complement to your meals. Again, a small amount cooked lightly is okay. Large amounts will disturb the digestion. Use a sprinkling of seeds in your favorite vegetable preparation for additional flavor and nutrients. Sesame seeds are high in calcium and easily assimilated if chewed well. Hemp seeds are quite heating, therefore not recommended for those with excess pitta.

Dried fruits such as raisins, cranberries, blueberries, papaya, coconut, mango, apricots, etc., are a good source of nutrients. Dried fruits are concentrated and are best when they are reconstituted (soaked in water). If you tend toward constipation or excess vata, avoid dried fruits unless cooked or reconstituted.

The list of available **fresh fruits** is very long and depends on your locale. Eat what is in season and grown locally. Explore the many options at your local farmers' market or health food store. Eat most fruit separate from other foods since they digest quickly and will ferment if detained in the digestive tract. Combining fruit with high-protein foods that take longer to digest results in gas, digestive upset, lack of assimilation of nutrients, and ama. For specific fruit suggestions, see the section in Ayurvedic Food Classification on choosing foods according to your dosha.

Include a variety of **fresh vegetables** in your daily meals that are most appropriate for your dosha and primarily sattvic. Eat fresh vegetables that are in season and locally grown. Prepare fresh vegetables by cutting, chopping, or grating, and eat them lightly cooked. Eat them in combination with grains, spices, and herbs for a tremendous variety of possibilities.

Fresh, dark leafy greens such as kales, collards, and some of the spicy greens are a significant element in keeping the body cleansed and balanced. Root vegetables such as carrots, beets, celery root, fennel, parsnips, and turnips are grounding, tasty, and augmenting, or adding to the body.

Minimize or avoid nightshade vegetables. Some of the most common vegetables served in restaurants are the nightshades: potato, tomato, eggplant and bell peppers. They are rajas, contributing to over activity of the mind. This change alone can make a significant difference in how you feel. Restaurants serve them because they are cheap, easy to store and transport and strong tasting—not because they are the healthiest for you. If you have joint or digestive problems, eliminate the nightshade vegetables and see if it helps reduce the problem. In the Yoga tradition, consuming nightshades is discouraged as they reduce vitality and dull the mind. People often ask if this includes sweet potatoes; it does not. Sweet potatoes are a different plant: they digest easily and are quite nutritious.

Eating only **raw foods** has become quite the popular approach these days. In warm environments and for certain constitutions (pitta predominant) this can work. For most people agni is not strong enough to digest the raw food and particularly when living in cold environments. Warm, cooked foods work best for the majority of people. You may find warm cooked foods work best for you in winter and that you enjoy a little raw food in summer midday while the sun is high in the sky to support agni. Avoid raw foods if you have any digestive problems.

What you **drink** makes a significant difference in how your body feels. Your body is mostly made of water and even mild dehydration will seriously weaken the body and affect the function of the mind. When your body is hydrated with lively, clean, room-temperature or slightly warm water and plenty of high-water-content food (fresh fruits and vegetables), the immune system is better able to do its job. It will be capable of warding off imbalance and disease. Moderation is key as with most things. Too much water weakens agni and aggravates vata dosha.

Ice water or any cold food or drink reduces agni and impairs digestion. As you might guess, any drink with carbonation, sugar, preservatives, caffeine, and other chemicals contributes to significant imbalance and poor health. Lacking prana, these substances are tamas in nature and contribute to dehydration.

Freshly made juice is a refreshing drink. Choose fruit or vegetables that are appropriate to your constitution and season. Fresh juices are concentrated, so cutting them in half with water or an herbal tea is best. Fruit digests quickly, so eat it at least three hours away from other food for optimal digestion.

Aloe vera juice is balancing for all doshas, and Ayurveda recognizes its extensive healing properties. Useful for restoring the lining of the intestines, and balancing the female reproductive system, it contains the bitter, astringent, pungent, and sweet tastes. The vipak, or post-digestive effect, is also sweet. One half cup to one cup each day is very helpful in relieving premenstrual and menopausal symptoms as well as digestive upsets.

In moderation, herbal teas are a reasonable alternative to water and fresh juice. Be aware that mold collects in herbal mixtures, particularly tea bags. If you suffer from allergies or sinus problems, drinking moldy herbal tea could be contributing. Use herbal teas made only from fresh herbs and see if it makes a difference. It may take some time for your system to rebalance. There may be other factors influencing allergies, such as food combinations, emotions, and chemical sensitivity.

Life is not about satisfying your every pleasure. Look at the results you manifest from that kind of thinking. Typically, it keeps you running from one thing to the next, looking for a depth of experience that is not there. Put love, gratitude, and caring attention into your food preparation. It makes a noticeable difference in your digestion and enjoyment of the meal. Remain conscious about the connection between what you eat and how you feel.

THE PROCESS OF EATING AND DRINKING

When you want to make a change in how you do something, become truly willing at all levels to give up the old way. Actively replace it with something new. This requires exploration, processing feelings, releasing old beliefs that are driving your attachment to the old ways, and discovery. Attachments and expectations keep you stuck and suffering. Clear the mind using breathing practices, meditation, and contemplation. Stay in this moment. This will help you begin the refocusing of your mind regarding the process of eating.

If overeating or compulsive eating is a problem for you, utilizing simple practices on a daily basis will help you heal the underlying disturbance. Refocus the mind to work in your best interest. This does not mean the mind will be perfectly void of all compulsive or crazy thoughts. They will come and they will go when you ignore them and let go. As a result of this step, you will develop a greater sense of yourself, being more in touch with your intuition.

Your higher self will guide you to what is in your best interest, beyond what your mind might tell you. If you find your mind holding out with a voice in the background telling you "We can go back to the old way after a while of this new stuff," or "Just be good for a while, and then you can eat everything you want," you have an opportunity for more clearing and healing. Laugh at yourself. Be completely honest with yourself. Let go of the old thinking. Letting go requires releasing the underlying feelings and beliefs that drive the old thinking.

The media, film, television, and fictional literature often promote emotional eating and drinking. The answer to any problem appears to be consumption of some sort. If you approach life this way, you will need to relearn to eat at regular meal times and not in between.

Sitting down to a meal can be an emotional experience. It will often trigger childhood behaviors that do not support your digestion and well-being. Voices from the past sometimes emerge. Notice how you sit at the table and what you do when you are eating. Sitting sideways to the table rather than straight on is a common physical stance when avoiding feelings. The underlying thinking may be seeking a quick getaway and therefore not allowing too much intimacy to happen. If this happens to you take time away from the table to process the feelings through journaling and possibly talking it over with a trusted friend. Become a witness of yourself and life. Fire your internal judge—your lower ego. This will allow you the space and freedom to make the changes you would like. Do your best to eradicate unhealthy habits in your life by retraining your mind.

Eating fast is an unhealthy habit that contributes to ama in the system. It often starts as a child and continues into adult life. Eating fast is a result of the desire to:

- get away from discomfort at the dinner table,
- feel in control of unpredictable surroundings,
- feel a sense of self-control about fear and anger,
- get a second helping because there might not be enough,
- feel okay, "I need more time as there is not enough time for me to do what I have to do to be okay."

Earlier in my life, I experienced all of the above affecting me to some degree. I was not aware of these unconscious beliefs until I slowed down to look inside. You may experience some of these or others. This kind of thinking has many layers of ego and denial covering it. It may not be easy to admit. All of this thinking disturbs digestion and assimilation of nutrients. Disturbed digestion and undigested food in your bowel movements are indicators that you are not receiving the nutrients from what you are eating. Rushing in life feeds an illusion of self-importance and builds ego besides disturbing digestion.

The journey of changing your relationship to food and eating will renew your relationship to yourself and others. Sit straight toward the table and food. Be in relationship with it and with the others around the table. Initially this may be easier to work on alone.

If you are slouching over the table and food, something is blocking your enthusiasm and connection to yourself. Your digestion and assimilation are not going to go well lowering your energy level. You have lost the sacred connection to yourself and eating.

Another habit that interferes with your relationship to food and others is eating while standing up or on the run. Avoid this as well as eating in the car. As an adult, you may say that you stand to eat or eat in the car merely because you are in a hurry and there just is not enough time. This situation results from having a distorted perception of what is most important in your day. Sit down, take a few deep breaths, express appreciation for the food and allow yourself to experience the difference.

Not allowing enough time to nourish yourself does not make any sense in the larger picture. Life develops many difficulties when you are not taking care of your own basic needs. Exploring your underlying feelings and beliefs about eating may help you better understand the results you are experiencing.

Avoidance behaviors around eating become unconscious. You may not realize the connection between your underlying feelings and the results in your digestion and intimate relationships. If you want intimacy in relating and you find you are not achieving it, process and release the old feelings. You can use your breath to move the energy up and right out the top of your head. Identify and replace the beliefs driving the old behavior with your new attitude and beliefs.

Do not eat while you are upset. It leads to ama on all levels in your being.

Allow the feelings to come forth and process through them. Write them down or use your breath as a way to release them. If you find you are still disturbed inside let the meal wait until you calm yourself.

If you are uncertain about processing feelings, observe people whom you admire for their health and well-being. Watch or ask them how they do it. Using the dosha guidelines in consideration of your own constitution gives you a reasonable point of reference. Use this rather than what the media or tradition has to offer and observe and respect your results. As you learn to be aware of your results, you will consciously make shifts to new ways. Your direct experience is most important. Lasting change is then available to you.

Abandon the habit of viewing eating and drinking as mechanical or something to rush through. Be attentive inside before eating. Allow yourself to develop a loving, creative, dynamic relationship with yourself, your food, and your surroundings. These fluid relationships will bring you a deeper, richer life.

Come together with others in acceptance, gratitude, and love. Greet each person and creature as spirit. Allow the prana-filled food to lift you up even when you feel grumpy. An open and conscious attitude makes this possible. Eating with others in a clean, sweet place with a calm, positive atmosphere supports healthy digestion and therefore improved well-being.

CHEWING

Early in my exploration around food, I had gas after eating. I had developed ama in my system that showed up as pain in the joints, cellulite, and general fatigue. I was eating mostly fresh, organic food. After testing for allergies and eliminating foods that did not agree with me, I still had gas and digestive problems. It turned out that I was eating in a hurry and taking large bites. This, combined with inadequate chewing, inhibited the digestive process and resulted in problems with digestion.

At the time, this diagnosis sounded ridiculous to me. It took a few more years of physical discomfort before I was willing to accept that not chewing enough and eating too fast was affecting my overall well-being. I now find that laying down my eating utensil after each bite is most helpful for keeping me conscious in the process. I learned to chew to liquid and enjoy each moderately sized bite. If I am stimulated I will still occasionally count my chews to help keep a reasonable loving perspective for my digestion.

Since digestion begins with the enzymes in the mouth the food must be chewed to liquid mush to have the opportunity to mix with those enzymes. Start with ten and work to twenty or more chews for each bite, depending on the type of food. Keep a flexible and conscious attitude, not a rigid rule. Feel and enjoy the chewing. The purpose is to optimize your digestion and enjoyment of the present. Lay down your utensil after each bite while you chew. Eating consciously and at a reasonable pace will help calm your mind and support optimal digestion.

When you are ready to eat, look at the food and admire it at your deepest level. Be aware of the aroma, color, and textures. As you begin chewing the food, feel the texture. Enjoy it with all of your senses. In other words, be aware. Call your mind to this task. An amazing thing is happening. Eating with an open heart and chewing thoroughly is a big step to health and harmony. By chewing your food thoroughly, you will begin to slow down in your entire being. It will help your mind focus and settle down.

The mind is like a little puppy that needs training. Sit down, let go, and be conscious in what you are doing. This means no standing, reading, watching television, or engaging in distractions while you are eating. Practicing calm focus with your mind while eating will bring great enjoyment and benefit to your health. Give your body a chance to do what it knows how to do well. Give your mind a rest from distraction.

You may find it very difficult at first to slow down and chew thoroughly. Once you get past the initial challenge, you will experience the benefits. It will make a significant difference in how you feel after eating. Make it an exercise for you and your family and see what happens. You may encounter resistance, so make it playful and laugh at yourself. Then incorporate it as part of your regular balanced eating.

When you want to make a change of any habit, replace the old with the new. Focus on the new approach, ignoring the old habit.

Another unhealthy and perhaps disrespectful habit to replace is pouring condiments on food before you taste it. Think about it. What drives you: an unconscious habit or craving? Is your mind closed and unconscious? Give yourself an opportunity to taste the food. If it has no taste or seems empty then find some different food to eat.

OPTIMAL TIMES FOR EATING
The doshas of vata, pitta, and kapha discussed previously also apply to the twenty-four hours of the day.

The pitta time of day, when the digestive fire is highest for everyone, is 10:00 a.m. to 2:00 p.m. and 10:00 p.m. to 2:00 a.m. Thus, midday is ideal for digestion of the heaviest meal of the day. The overnight window is ideal for supporting your healing and rejuvenation while you sleep; it is not a time for eating or starting new activities. When you stay up past 10:00 p.m., you get a "second wind" because pitta has come up. Ideally, you would be in bed sleeping by ten. It may take some retraining to go to sleep by then, but the adjustment is worth the increased rest and sense of well-being that comes from having enough sleep.

The digestive fire is lower in the evening, so eat a lighter meal than midday. Complete the evening meal at least three hours before bed, allowing time for digestion. When you go to bed with undigested food in your system, digestion is almost stopped, resulting in grogginess and congestion in the morning.

Other things that draw energy away from your digestion are anger, anxiety, excessive fear, exercise and having sex. Do not participate in sex within two hours of eating. If you are anxious or angry about something, do not eat. Take time to sort through your feelings and eat at the next mealtime. Your mind thinks you will starve, not your body. Most of us do not suffer from starvation by lack of food. Our starvation is from lack of connection to our true self, which will have us look to food for comfort.

In this culture of mass media and affluence, using food in detrimental ways is common. Eating every time an urge pops into your mind disturbs both the body and mind. Allowing every twitch and desire of the mind to be satisfied continues to weaken the mind. This is why eating at regular times is so important. This does not mean being rigid. Make your mealtime a priority in your life and commit to a regular schedule that you follow. It means giving your body, mind, and spirit due respect. When you do not do this, you feed depression and illness. Once you recognize the problem and understand the new practices, taking one step at a time to change will help you see the benefits and validate your experience.

I hear people say, "I do not want to get too clean because then I will be too sensitive to handle the junk." In other words, I do not want to treat myself too well, so that it will be easier to treat myself badly whenever I want. This opens the door to a weak and disorderly mind, leading to suffering and disease in both the body and mind. When you are in balance, your immune system is strong: you will handle small insults very easily with little consequence.

OVERCOMING DESIRES AND THE MIND

Feeding the lower desires brings misery and suffering. It keeps us on a merry-go-round of disconnection, isolation, anxiety, depression, and acting out in an attempt to find some joy in life. The same cycle applies to food. How and what you eat may seem like "no big deal," and yet it has a more direct affect on all aspects of your life than anything else you do other than your thinking. Feeding your lower ego brings suffering—when you could be experiencing the joy, peace, and sweetness in life. The lower ego receives negative affirmation by not doing a good job of taking care of you. In order to live in serenity, continually turn in the new direction, away from the lower ego and desires.

People who eat large amounts of processed sugar all of their lives find it challenging to change. Refined sugar is addictive to the body and mind. When they decide to cut out refined sugar, they find themselves feeling victimized. When the time comes to move beyond victimization, look at the underlying feelings. Processing those feelings allows healing and real change to take place. Craving the sweet taste is often about avoiding feelings and not allowing in the sweetness of life. The underlying beliefs that generate feelings can change when you reveal them and let them go. Sometimes they are small, seemingly insignificant feelings. Exploring them and changing the underlying beliefs is transformative.

Freedom to be your true self is on the other side of those feelings. The process is most successful with the support of others in a similar healing process. When your system is out of balance, your attachments and fears will drive you to things you never imagined yourself doing in order to hang on to the old ways. Physical and mental addictions become your reality. You can temporarily curtail them with self-will, changes in habits, drugs, and various other methods. However, long-lasting relief from the cyclical insanity of craving and addiction is not likely. You must change the underlying beliefs and elicit the support of your Divine source within.

When you are learning how to focus and become the master of your mind and senses, be gentle and persistent. If you find this difficult, stop and ask yourself, "Why am I in such a hurry?" Notice the response and then be amused with yourself. If you are consuming any type of caffeine, sugar, or processed foods, your mind will be racing. This may be normal for you. However, a racing mind is not your natural state of being. Do not believe the game your mind plays, saying that you had better keep moving fast and doing in order to have value.

If you are cut off from your feelings, you may take on the lie that says, "If I can't see it or feel it, it is not there." Realize that consuming concentrated stimulants and heavily processed foods have a dramatic effect on your body and mind. The chemistry of your mind is a result of how you live and what you consume. Every habit or samskara can be healed. The effort required to do so depends on the depth of the impression and habit.

The connection between your body, mind, and spirit is subtle, sensitive, and glorious. Balance and harmony are a miracle available to you. This only happens when you connect to the deepest part of you and take charge of your mind. It might be appropriate to stop eating on occasion and process feelings by writing, talking, or just pausing. If you are anxious or angry, wait and eat when the emotional charge has dissipated. Light conversation or silence during meals best supports your digestion. You will find that you do not need to eat as much when you honor the process, eat consciously, and chew food thoroughly. You will feel light and energized after eating.

Acceptance and allowing peace to come in are the final steps in a harmonious relationship to food. Many people are concerned about whether or not their food contains "negative" energy. Negative energy is something to be aware of, and you can learn how to clear this energy by infusing the food with your love. However, your own internal resistance, anxiety, anger, and resentment will keep you from taking in the prana and nutrients that any food has to offer. A negative attitude will keep you from receiving the nourishment of the very best food. An attitude of appreciation will support lower-quality food in supplying you with some nourishment.

Bring a sacred attitude back into your eating and your food. Acknowledge the eternal exchange and movement of energy. Put your love into the food. Allow it in for yourself, and let it be available for others. You will find that you take a step up in your energy when you eat, rather than feeling over stimulated or sluggish afterward.

Whom you decide to eat with can make a significant difference in how you digest your food. Whether you are eating with friends, family, pets, or alone, find peace and acceptance with what you choose in life. Eating alone is healthy as long as you bring the sacred to the process and accept the present with joy. If you would like company, invite someone to share a meal with you. Ideally, everyone who eats together participates in the process of preparation and clean-up. This fosters a sense of community and security.

CLEANSING

The idea of "cleansing" has become very popular. Many people harm themselves with extremes in fasts and cleanses. They bounce right back to poor-quality food and poor eating practices. Taking an extreme action to cleanse when you are not yet willing to be attentive to what and how you are eating on a daily basis damages your mind, body, and overall health. People say to me, "But I feel so good while I am doing it." The contrast is particularly notable since they also feel "not so well" the rest of the time.

An extreme approach results in suppressed desires and blocked energy flow. Too much cleansing will deplete your vital resources, leaving you fearful and spacey. Cultivate a conscious approach to daily living that includes both nourishing and cleansing foods in a ratio of 60% nourishing, or augmenting, and 40% extractive, or cleansing. In my experience, cleansing and fasting without a devotional component is not successful in terms of long-lasting transformation to harmony and balance. When you push the mind to a sense of starvation, there is a significant rebound effect, resulting in overindulgence and feeding the lower ego. A devotional attitude keeps the mind focused on your source and abundance, taking you beyond the ego.

The practice of Ayurveda asks you to find the middle ground and not be extreme. Suggestions for cleansing vary according to your constitution, the season, and your health. A simple *kitchadi* (pronounced "kichari") dish works well for a gentle cleansing. Kitchadi is a soupy combination of basmati rice, split mung beans, spices, and herbs cooked with ghee to engage their healing effects. It may also have vegetables added.

You can modify the kitchadi to support particular doshas or organs of the body by changing the vegetables and spices used. Notice the color, amounts, odors, and other qualities of your elimination. Use the principle of opposite brings balance to give you an idea of how to adjust the kitchadi.

The cleansing tastes are pungent (e.g., ginger), bitter (e.g., leafy greens) and astringent (e.g., beans and squash). To enhance the cleansing qualities of food in general, steam, boil, and make soups. Foods that are heavier and more congestive are dairy products, meat, and flour. Dairy in an appropriate form and amount is nourishing.

Let go of fears about fixing your body and focus on providing the support it needs to do its job. Eat 60% nourishing augmenting foods and 40% cleansing extractive foods on a daily basis to provide that support. Cleansing as part of a balanced approach to consumption brings harmony and clarity to your life.

FOOD COMBINING

Food combinations are a major factor in your well-being. It's most important to realize that a poor combination of foods is detrimental to agni and therefore your ability to digest and assimilate nutrients from food. Harmonious food combining makes a significant difference in agni's ability to do its job and consequently in how you feel.

Poor food combinations inhibit the effectiveness of digestive enzymes and reduce your agni's ability to digest. The body and mind will adapt to poor food combinations and leads to disease. Drinking orange juice with milk and cereal, for example, is a major assault to agni resulting in symptoms of gas, indigestion, bad breath, and body odor, among others. Some people think these symptoms are a normal part of living, or that the problem comes from a malfunction of the body. Having a lot of gas or feeling sluggish after eating a meal is an indication of a problem with what and/or how you ate. If you are having a problem, consider the combination of foods you ate, as well as what you ate. Eating too large a quantity of any food also causes problems with gas and digestion.

Ayurveda regards each food as having its own taste(s), energy (heating or cooling), and vipak, or post-digestive effect. Combining two or more foods possessing different tastes, energies, and post-digestive effects is confusing for your agni. The result is fermentation, putrefaction, gas, and ama in the body and mind. Eating poor combinations of heavy foods reduces agni and slows digestion. The food remains in the digestive tract too long, leaving you feeling heavy. Eating the same foods separately could actually result in the opposite effect: stimulate agni and help burn ama out of your system.

Ayurveda suggests the following related to food combining:

- Eat fruits as their own meal separate from other food. For example if meals are 5-6 hours apart a piece of fruit at least two hours from other food may be okay.

- Allow for complete digestion of the previous meal 4-6 hours, before eating again.
- Eat melons alone, not with any other food, or leave them alone. They digest very quickly and if slowed by other food fermentation will take place causing disturbed digestion.
- Avoid combining milk or yogurt with citrus, bananas, or sour fruit. The dairy will curdle in the stomach.
- Avoid eating equal amounts of honey and ghee together.
- Avoid eating two foods together that are contradictory in their action. For example, meat that is heating with coconut or milk that is cooling.

You can do your own research and problem solving by removing certain foods from your diet or by eating a particular food alone. If you are having a problem, remove the suspicious food from your meal and see if the symptom(s) are gone. If they are, later try eating that particular food alone and see if the symptoms return. To do this effectively, be certain that you digest fully whatever you last ate, at least four to six hours earlier. The section Overeating and Struggles with Weight Control in the Problems and Answers chapter includes a method to see if your digestion is complete. Do not eat for at least two to four hours after eating the suspicious food. If there is a problem with this food, it may take a long time for digestion to complete. Observe how you feel in the next twenty-four hours.

Next, learn to combine foods in ways that promote agni and efficient assimilation of nutrients. Eating foods combined to optimize digestion helps you move away from cravings and disease toward balance. In general, follow the guidelines above. Learn to recognize the effects that different foods and beverages have on your body and mind and make wise choices. Of course chewing the food thoroughly is critical in this process.

Sorting out what is right for you is an interesting and discriminating process. In the beginning, you may feel like there will be nothing left to eat. Keep going. The food choices available are numerous, even when balancing your doshas. Your shift in perspective will amaze you once you embrace the results in how you feel.

Be attentive to your choices and actions, take responsibility, and know what you are eating. When you eat something that does not agree with you, drinking half a cup to a cup of aloe vera juice will help to restore the lining of your intestines. Identify where you went unconscious in your behavior so that you can recognize that point in the future and take a different action. Say "no thanks" if you are not clear about a food or a combination of foods. Eating food prepared by someone you do not know is unpredictable and not ideal. Eating food that you or someone you know has prepared is best. The attitude and energy of the cook goes into the food.

Getting Started

FINDING ANSWERS

Answers to the problems concerning conscious consumption of food and drink begin with your relationship to yourself. Many people today are clamoring for a sense of connection without knowing how to get it. Are you searching for a feeling of community, a partner, and meaningful relationships? All of these connections are available to you. Through raising your consciousness and bringing the sacred back to your eating, you will regain a sense of feeling whole. Realize that you need not do everything presented to you. Again, you can say "no thanks" to some things. Focus on a few substantive activities that lead you in the direction that you want to go. This approach applies to eating, drinking, and any other activity in life.

Fear is what takes us off track. The fear of missing something, the fear of not being enough in the world, and the fear of not having enough will drive your behavior until you become uncomfortable and miserable enough to change. Do not wait for this to happen. You can begin to wake up and make different choices, now. This is the beginning of responsible consumption and spiritual living.

Engaging in these practices is a place to begin:

- Let go of thinking you "should" or "need" to know what is coming next in life. Look for ways you may be hiding this attitude from yourself and let them go.
- Surrender moment by moment to your Divine source, that which gives you a deeper connection to your true sense of self.
- Allow that power to be the foundation for your living.
- Rely on your source both when difficulties come up in life and when things are great. This is the beginning of the true practice of faith.
- Give up coercing, resisting, and struggling. Accept life as it is.
- Forgive and move on for your own freedom.
- Let your trust and connection to self give you direction, rather than your defenses.

Many people say, "Eat well and you will be healthier." Possibly, yet this is not the total picture. The body is a representation of what and *how* you consume such things as food, drink, cosmetics, chemicals, and attitudes. Unconscious consumption affects your attitude and the cycle of life. Your unity with all of life becomes disturbed.

Consider the possibility that you are eternal spirit that is unchanging, no matter what is happening to the body. If you block your sense of spirit by what and how you are consuming, you block your access to the source of power within. Your conscious, ongoing connection to your spirit brings the greatest radiance, beauty, and well-being to your body, no matter what its condition. Your sense of internal connection and unity is critical to health, peace, and joy-filled living.

Thinking you must do everything at once is an idea rooted in perfectionism and will lead to feeling overwhelmed. Give it up; it reduces your self confidence.

Accept your reality today and each day, and allow for a continual growth of perspective. Each time you feel anxious or overwhelmed, say to yourself, "I don't have to do everything at once. Everything I need for this moment will be provided. I can live each moment as it comes." Then, focus on the next step right in front of you.

Make small changes gradually to develop greater confidence. The result will be greater consciousness in your consumption and a greater sense of your connection to the universe. From that point, you can be in peace no matter what is going on around you.

Practicing faith is the foundation of spiritual living. Faith is a trust in the process of divine source energy. It is a reliance on a higher reality. Whatever your faith is in—call it God, Christ, Buddha, Allah, Supreme Being, Great Spirit, the universal consciousness, mother nature, your higher self, or whatever—surrender is the key. By surrendering, I mean letting go of the idea of controlling or knowing the outcomes in your life. Surrender to that deepest place within you, not to rules someone else gives you.

Faith takes place in the unknown. It will help you discover your connection to your higher self. The willingness to surrender self-will, to allow yourself to feel a part of something bigger, will support you and guide you in your life journey.

Embrace the reality of your beliefs and feelings. They create your results in life. Remember that you are always the creator of your own reality. Become willing to go inside to make real change. You will find your truth and your inner voice. This is the process of spiritualizing your life. In my experience, this spiritual component is necessary for a solid foundation for living.

Be attentive to your behavior in all areas of life, in particular to anything you put in and on your body. Consciousness about food and your relationship to it ensures you make choices that are in your own best interest, not just to please others, to look good, or to "do it right."

If you participate in a religion, find the component that touches your spirit most deeply. You may choose to find that connection without a religion. The study of sacred texts and contemplating how they apply in your life can nourish your soul. This could be as simple as a daily reading of a few lines. Take a moment to see how the reading applies in your life. It does not require spending a lot of time; however, a focused moment will make a difference in your life.

The devotional aspects of practice are the acts that bring about the remembrance of spirit. It may be a prayer or mantra, or whatever form works for you. For some people, prayer is spoken or chanted, for others prayer is only internal. It may include other rituals and acknowledgements. The important thing is to find something simple that you are willing to do on a regular basis that touches you deeply.

Acknowledging gratitude and honoring your food and all that comes to you is a phenomenal place to begin.

All you need to do to get started is make a decision. Make your inner journey a priority in life. You will find joy, community, and wonder by living in concert with nature rather than at odds with it. Leading a joy-filled life through conscious consumption requires saying "no" sometimes, doing less, simplifying, and focusing clearly and consistently on what you choose in your life.

The subtle aspects in life are much more influential than the gross. In other words, the seemingly little things in life and the energy behind what you see are generally the most important. Be attentive to the essence of what you are doing and how you are living and it will help you be clear with yourself.

WHAT CHANGES TO EXPECT

As you incorporate changes in your thinking, food selections, and preparation, embrace realistic expectations. Make a plan and let go of the timing of results. Take small steps. Allow them to integrate and become a part of your living. Add changes gradually, such as only having food that is fresh and non-processed, changing attitudes about certain foods so that you may add something new, or changing a particular eating ritual. Remember, you cannot find your innermost self and unity while keeping the old ways intact. If you could have, you already would have. If you file away the old ways for later use or "keep them just in case," you will go back to them and get the old results.

Your attitudes are how you carry your energy. They represent your defenses, opinions, and suppressed patterns of behavior. Energy moves naturally. With clear intention, you can intentionally move your own energy and work through suppressed patterns to a more balanced life.

Take changes one step at a time. Work through the feelings of loss, resentment, anger, and grief. These feelings may come up even though you want to release the old ways. They are common even when the change is obviously great and in your best interest. Feel and acknowledge your feelings. Experience them and let them pass. They will pass if you let them. Do not try to change them, "stuff them," or eat over them to feel better. They are your experience but it does not mean they are correct. They are often incorrect. Instead, maintain an open mind and acknowledge that these feelings may be resistance to change. Fear is the basis of these feelings: fear of not getting what you want or fear of losing something you possess. For example, you may want to stop eating refined sugar. You may experience fears of not being a part of celebrations, not getting "treats," or not connecting with family. You may also be concerned about offending others. Release the fears. Replace them each time you are aware of them with faith. Do this through willingness and simple daily practices.

While working with a family with three young children, I found the best approach was with gradual changes. Their food and eating choices were leading to frequent illness and other health problems. Over the course of a couple of years, they had switched from a diet high in refined sugar to a much smaller quantity of naturally sweetened products. Mom sometimes felt anxious about the slow change. Then a relative came to visit and inadvertently showed her how far the family had come.

She had found a naturally sweetened yogurt that the whole family enjoyed. She offered their new favorite snack to her mother-in-law, who thought it was awful and wouldn't eat it—it wasn't sweet enough. She shared this story with me because it helped her realize how much her family's taste buds and perspective had changed. Be aware of the signs that show you your progress.

Acknowledge your attitude about what you are consuming. Slow down and enjoy. Right where you are is the most important place to be. Be persistent and be gentle. Learn to be with others while eating in a calm, considerate way without straying from your path. This is the beginning of a new kind of self-care and nurturing. Be aware and take responsibility for yourself. Learn to listen to your body and feelings. You will develop a new level of self-honesty and greater honesty with others. It will show in your bright eyes and clear skin!

You may find that you are enjoying a healthy relationship with food, and then slip back to old ways. If your system has become strong and balanced, one insult will be noticeable, but with small, if any, consequences. It may be easy to fall into thinking, "the old stuff may not have been so bad." This will lead you quickly back to old patterns. You will notice the effects more when your system is weak and out of balance, since your body is not able to handle the insult as easily.

Consistency in your new routine will strengthen the mind and improve your ability to deal with life in a peaceful manner. Discipline increases your steadiness, perseverance, and courage. These attributes are not cultivated in mainstream culture. They require honestly stepping into your own life. If the idea of discipline and consistency sounds silly to you, realize that you are merely worrying about what other people think. When you are ready to let go of what others think, you are ready for the next step toward freedom.

Acting on self-indulgent impulses weakens the will. Turning away from such impulses is the first step in strengthening the will. The next step is a committed focus in your new direction and recognition of small successes. This strength of will shows up as perseverance and endurance that lead you through challenges. Learn to identify with your spiritual self, which includes the will, and not with the physical body that is ever deteriorating.

Make some reminders to place in your daily path that express your new chosen attitudes and sentiments that support your new behaviors. Make one new attitude on a card and put them in your car, on your desk, on your refrigerator, and next to your bed. Contemplate them each day.

Notice if your habits are toward the negative and not letting in the beauty of life. Making the shift will require consciously letting go of the old negative ways and refocusing on the sweetness and wonder of life.

A student shared his story about turning away from the old ways while on a construction job site. He said no to pizza with the guys because he knew that eating it would make him feel bad afterward. Although part of him really wanted the pizza, he felt good afterward because he was not dealing with the negative effects. He strengthened the positive use of his will. Each step makes a difference, and they accumulate over time bringing strength to the mind and connection to the higher self.

Practice consciously and change will come to you. Notice your results. Validate the changes for yourself. This does not mean brag about how great you are. It means to clearly acknowledge to yourself the changes. Then pause to allow the connection to your deepest self to flourish.

This is not about punishment, grades, or judgment. Beating yourself up after eating junk food will keep you in the cycle that compelled you initially. Let go of the old ways. They serve only the part of your ego that takes you away from your truth.

Learning to say no to the desires that do not serve your well-being is a tremendous step in healing and strengthening the mind. Start small. As a desire comes up, ask yourself, "If I take action in this desire, does it serve my well-being and spirit?" You will cultivate your personal power each time you ask this question and make a decision that considers your mind, body, and spirit connection a priority. Other questions to ask are "What does eating this food offer me?" And then "What is actually provided?" Is it five minutes of pleasure, excess weight, and disrupted sleep? Or you could ask yourself "Does eating this take me in the direction I want to go, connect me to my higher self and others, assist me in feeling balanced and harmonious? Over time, this process will become natural and clear, and a sense of grace and balance will come into your life.

Turning away from desires is not about being rigid or denying. Instead, sort through the parts of your living that do not serve your best interest and eliminate them. Each action in your life either takes you toward your innermost self or away from it. Take responsibility for your mind and your life so that you can live fully.

Recognize yourself as a part of the whole. Begin to see yourself in unity with life, including all of nature, plants, animals, insects, and children. When you recognize that life is more than seeking your pleasures, you can begin to allow in the possibilities of being a part of the whole. When you are only seeking to fulfill your desires and your ego is driving your thoughts and actions, no space is available for unity, joy and peace.

Here are ways to encourage unity, joy and peace in your life:

- Pause and be truly present, noticing this moment.
- Listen to the sounds or silence around you.
- Feel the texture of the air and the energy around you.
- Be aware of your breathing and the fragrances around you.
- Listen to children and be present with them.
- Be with plants and animals in a conscious way, with all of your senses.
- Allow yourself to deeply experience the sunrise and sunset without talking.
- Follow the moon as it moves through its cycle and realize how you are a part of the cycle.
- Take long walks in nature, being aware of your surroundings.
- Cultivate an overall attitude of appreciation by making a list of the things you are grateful for on a daily or weekly basis.
- Meditate daily; even five minutes mindfully focused on stillness will make a difference.
- Pray in any conscious way, anytime.

An effective way to develop unity and peace in your life is to commit to one daily practice or action (such as those listed above) and be aware of how you feel during and after this practice. Then, add a second practice three weeks later.

If you get off track or find yourself resistant, acknowledge this and return to the practice with a willingness to begin again. Stay with it.

This is not a performance. Give up grading or criticizing yourself. You only feed the ego when you are rigid and critical with yourself. Notice if your real motive is about what other people think of you. This common motive underlies unconscious behaviors and leads to great suffering.

With gentle persistence, you will observe significant changes in a very short amount of time. When practiced regularly, your new tools will be available and especially helpful during times of stress. As you cultivate your connection and learn to call on your source of power, you can be a responsible participant in your life's direction. The unlimited potential is there for you. Stay conscious and call on it.

A survey taken of business people who are successful in terms of family, career, and community found that, in all cases, these people took extended time for inner reflection. They felt it helped them make better decisions as they allowed their intuition to flourish. One participant commented that as he did less in life there was more space for his divine source to be present, which led him to make better decisions in all of life.

As you begin to live more consciously, you will see the places where you are unconscious in your consumption. Make changes gradually, as you are truly willing. Do not try to force a change. It will not work. Validate your own experience, listen to others with an open mind, and make your own decisions.

You will begin to gravitate toward eating, drinking, and consuming that is in your best interest as spirit, rather than satisfying fleeting pleasures.

At first, discovering how little conscious thought you have in this part of your living can be startling and challenging. With perseverance, increased consciousness will quickly become a welcome addition to your life.

As you begin to make changes, friends and family may try to sabotage your efforts. They may continue to serve you food and drink you already told them you no longer wish to have. They may make fun of you for being different. They are usually not aware of the impact and potential harm their actions and words can inflict; unconsciousness and their own insecurity are behind this kind of behavior. Remember, their behavior toward you most likely reflects discomfort with their own choices and have nothing to do with you. Continue your path anyway. Sometimes the changes in you will inspire them to improvements.

Clearing past impressions is part of the process of change. They accumulate over time, and it may feel like these impressions, or ruts, engulf your life. Falling into these ruts may be familiar. Healing the impressions that impede your connection to your source will bring you great joy and peace.

Practice harmonious living on the inside, and you will express it freely on the outside.

Allowing growth in one area of life opens you to the possibilities of growing in many others. Intentional changes that help you to connect to food and the process of eating will translate to other areas of life. You can face life head on and work with the wonderful opportunities available to you. Alternatively, you can sit back, be miserable, take medications to numb you from life, and let it pass by in unconsciousness. As such an integral part of living, consumption of food and drink is an obvious place to begin. Bringing consciousness to the process of eating connects you to yourself, the earth, and all of nature.

Problems and Answers

The body and mind are your primary tools for experience in this life. The body has many functions that are very useful to you in your self-care. The tendency to ignore it, treat it like a machine, or dote on it in ways that promote imbalance is quite common.

Behavior around food and eating is a habitual inheritance that changes little until you bring consciousness to your actions. Some people inherit health problems. Others accrue problems from environmental pollutants. These problems can seem unsolvable. This may or may not be true, but you can significantly affect your well-being through the choices you make around food and eating. Many hereditary issues and environmental sensitivities fall to the background with conscious, healthy life choices around consumption. The body and spirit work together in harmony when you let them. They acknowledge and support your connection to self.

The following are simple, natural ways to work with your body, mind, and spirit. They are a first step toward solving many problems. If you work with them, they will assist you in developing a further understanding of how and why your body and mind respond as they do to your food and lifestyle. Other supportive practices mentioned in this book will help and sometimes Ayurvedic herbs may be necessary.

Although the name of this chapter is Problems and Answers, remember that Yoga and Ayurveda are not about treating symptoms, but about rooting out the cause and making long-lasting change for wellness and longevity. The suggestions listed have some variations, but there is a consistent foundation in all of them. Fixing symptoms in order to keep doing everything else the same way is not the intention. Keep the ultimate goal of balance and connection in your mind. I hope that this chapter will help you see your connection with everything inside and outside of you. I suggest that you read all of the sections even if you don't identify with the title. You may discover some helpful tools for you or someone you know.

Blood Sugar Fluctuation

Blood sugar problems are often the result of consuming refined sugar, caffeine, and processed foods that disturb digestion and prohibit assimilation of other food, such as protein. Eating large amounts of sweets feeds the intense desire to eat sweets continuously, promoting diabetes and obesity. The physical body becomes so imbalanced that blood sugar peaks and drops in response to too much sugar consumption. Furthermore, this cycle often results in an overgrowth of yeast in the intestines, as well as many other imbalances that contribute to a fluctuating blood sugar. When the lining of the intestines is out of balance, agni is disturbed. The hormones in the body become imbalanced, resulting in exaggerated emotions and the loss of a sense of self.

The first step to help balance your system is to include about one half cup of preservative-free aloe juice morning and evening in your diet. Eliminate any added sugar, processed foods, refined grains (pasta, couscous), caffeine, and alcohol. These items are all significant in problems with blood sugar fluctuation. Have a piece of fruit as an alternative to acting on the desire for sweets. Include cooked whole grains in your eating daily and other foods that pacify vata to alleviate the fear of blood sugar fluctuation. See the section on Digestive Problems regarding eating all day long.

Dosha Imbalance

- Vata in excess
- Pitta possibly in excess
- Kapha sometimes in excess

Sections to Reference

- Appendix A recipes
- Digestive Problems
- Ayurvedic Food Classification
- Letting Go of the Illusion of Control

CONSTANT FATIGUE AND SICKNESS

I included this section because it is a stage in a progressive process of disease formation. If you are feeling constant fatigue and are often sick with colds or the flu, your living is compromising your immune system and there is imbalance. Many people don't realize how sick and tired they are because it becomes "normal." There is frequently some denial about how often one is actually not feeling well or sick.

Cleaning up how you are eating and living is the most comprehensive way to clear up these problems with long-term success. Disturbance in your elimination is likely, meaning diarrhea or constipation. The result is toxins backing up into your system causing fatigue and susceptibility to pathogens. Cutting out refined sugar, processed foods, caffeine, and alcohol will make a good start. Stop taking supplements that claim to give you more energy. Let the body heal and readjust to its natural function.

Most often vata is in excess. The tendency for the other doshas to be out of balance will vary according to your own constitution and way of living. If you are thin and tired, you will do best with warm, cooked, nourishing foods, including plenty of ghee or appropriate oil with your food. If you are overweight and are having these problems, fresh foods, soups, and small amounts of oils will help; no sweets. A moderate walk after eating will also help. In all cases, avoid stimulants such as sugar, alcohol, and caffeine since they will dehydrate you and drain your energy. Eating a sattvic diet with selected rajasic foods that support strengthening your agni will be most healing.

Dosha Imbalance

- Vata in excess
- Kapha deficiency is possible if you are very thin, and possibly pitta in excess

Sections to Reference

- Constipation and Dehydration
- Digestive Problems
- Conscious Consumption
- Food Combining
- The Process of Eating and Drinking

CONSTIPATION AND DEHYDRATION

Constipation in your body is similar to not emptying the trashcan in your house. Things turn sour, rot, make an unpleasant odor, and promote an environment for pathogens. The same process happens in your mind. Constipation is the result of poor eating, dehydration, holding on to emotions, unhealthy lifestyle, and lack of exercise. Poor eating includes overeating, under-eating, eating before the previous meal has fully digested, eating at inappropriate times, and imbalanced food choices.

Adequate hydration and elimination are necessary to keep you in balance. Having two to four bowel movements each day is a healthy range. Ideally, they would be first thing in the morning and about twenty minutes after each main meal. If this is not happening and you had normal amounts of food the day before, you are constipated.

Constipation is typically associated with dehydration. Dehydration is a component of most serious illnesses. It has become the normal way of operating for many people. It may also show up as a pattern of constipation and diarrhea.

You must drink water and be hydrated in order to taste and experience the balancing essence of the food you eat. Drink fresh, clean water each day. Make sure your water is clean of pollutants and as prana-filled as possible.[3] This critical step makes a difference in your health and well-being. By following these few steps, your elimination will become more regular. If your body is not eliminating effectively (producing urine, feces, and sweat), ama is accumulating. In addition, the skin becomes dry and flakey.

Consume water warm or at room temperature for optimal digestion and balance in your system. Avoid drinking cold water. It reduces your agni and contributes to imbalance.

First thing in the morning, rinse your mouth with a cup of warm water and then drink a cup of warm water. After a night of sleep, the body's reserves need to replenish with water. This stimulates elimination and prepares the digestive tract for the meal to come. This is also a nice time to gargle with warm water to remove excess kapha.

Drink about ½ cup of water twenty to thirty minutes before each meal and before exercising. You may not eat as much when you can distinguish between thirst and hunger. Drinking water before a meal rather than during encourages more thorough chewing. It also eliminates the possibility of washing food down. Eat slowly to improve your digestion and enjoy the meal.

Drink ½ cup of water during meals if desired. Do not drink large amounts of water or other liquids with or right after a meal. It dilutes your digestive enzymes and disturbs the digestive process. Drinking about a one half cup of room temperature or warm water about every hour helps keep an even consumption of water throughout the day, maintaining hydration and supporting optimal digestion. A healthy colon is a hydrated colon. In any disease, imbalance in the colon is a factor, often because of dehydration.

Do not consume excessive amounts of water or other fluids. It stresses the kidneys and washes out valuable nutrients. For some people this causes loose stool and continued dehydration. Too much of anything will create imbalance. Consistency is important. Drink about 1 liter of water per day, depending on your level of activity and your living environment.

If you are constipated, add a small amount of flax meal to your food to support healthy elimination. Eating fresh fruits and vegetables helps provide the water content needed to stay hydrated. Take a comfortable walk of a hundred to a thousand steps at a moderate pace after eating to assist digestion—not a vigorous walk. Do not recline right after eating as it disturbs digestion, contributing to constipation.

Any of the vegetable or kitchadi recipes in this book would be helpful in transitioning to a new way of eating. Keep your consumption of drying foods to a minimum. Avoid most beans (split or whole mung beans are okay), crackers, and salads.

Dosha Imbalance

- Vata in excess
- Pitta possibly in excess
- Kapha could be excess or deficient

Sections to Reference

- Conscious Consumption
- Ayurvedic Food Classification
- Appendix A, kitchadi recipes

- The Process of Eating and Drinking
- Digestive Problems
- Stiff and Aching Joints

DIGESTIVE PROBLEMS

Disturbed digestion creates ama. The result is strong, sometimes sour, body odor and skin problems such as acne. Many people who eat good-quality, balanced food still have toxic body odor. This may be a result of ama in their system. When agni is weak or out of balance, you are much more subject to candida overgrowth, pathogens, and disease.

The body clearly reflects poor digestion in many ways, such as dull hair, weak fingernails, skin blemishes and rashes, poor coloring, and strong body odor. Acne on the face, neck, and upper back are also indicators of poor digestion. The upper back muscles just above and between the shoulder blades can become spastic and quite painful when the digestion is disturbed.

There are some very important points to consider for strengthening agni and optimal digestion. Many people today suffer from problems with digestion and treat them with various drugs or natural remedies. Rushing and running—particularly around meals—is common. One simple factor that disturbs digestion is fast and inadequate chewing. Food not thoroughly chewed is not readily digestible. The saliva must have an opportunity to mix with the food to allow the enzymes to initiate the digestive process. Poor combinations of foods are another important contributor to digestive problems.

Breakfast comes from the notion of "breaking the fast" after sleeping. Something light and simple is enough. Give your body an opportunity to wake up. Ideally, have breakfast at seven in the morning or later. If you do heavy physical work, a larger breakfast may be appropriate. In any case, do not choose a sugary breakfast.

If your meal from the night before has not completely digested, you will feel sluggish in the morning. Adding more food or stimulants such as caffeine to try to "energize" for the day are common approaches that cause imbalance and weaken agni. The result is initial stimulation followed by more heaviness and weaker agni. Using stimulants or sugary sweets will send your body into a detrimental pattern of craving and dehydration.

When you observe your digestion, consider how you are digesting life on the outside as well. Resisting the reality of your life (in other words, not digesting your life) disrupts the digestion of food. Digestion of life on the outside and inside goes hand in hand. When one aspect of digestion becomes disturbed, the other will follow shortly.

Often digestive problems are not from the malfunctioning body but from a negative attitude. If you want to eliminate problems with digestion, address the real issues at hand rather than spending money to give your body a drug or supplement to try to force it to behave better. Physical symptoms are your body's way of communicating an underlying problem. Supporting the body while you go through a transition is helpful, but addressing the real issues of digestion on all levels will lead you to harmony and balance. Providing your body with the opportunity to do what it naturally knows how to do builds esteem. Your attitude is the most powerful force.

Allowing enough time for digestion, eating easily digested cooked food, and no late-night eating are critical changes to improve the strength of your digestion.

Dosha Imbalance

- Vata or kapha in excess with slow digestion
- Pitta in excess with heartburn

Sections to Reference

- The Process of Eating and Drinking
- Food Combining
- Adding New Foods to Your Diet

GROGGINESS UPON WAKING AND FOOD HANGOVERS

Waking up groggy and food hangovers result in a sluggish mind and body. Many people experience this regularly. The most common causes are poor-quality food, poor combinations of food, food allergies often created by the previous two items, overeating in one sitting, eating too close to the previous meal, and eating too close to bedtime. All of these behaviors reduce agni, leading to ama in your system. The result is that you will not feel well.

Eating moderate amounts of fresh, dosha-appropriate food at least three hours before going to bed will make a big difference in how you feel in the morning. If your digestion is slow, allow even more time between the last meal of the day and going to bed. Your sleep will be more peaceful, and you will awaken refreshed. Digestion weakens and ama increases when you eat before the previous meal has completely digested. Allowing enough time between meals will allow you to maintain strong agni.

Changing these behaviors will allow you to avoid post-holiday illnesses. Most illness after holidays occurs because of overeating, poor-quality food, poor food combinations, and consumption of excessive amounts of sugar and alcohol. When agni is compromised and weak, your system cannot handle even a small insult from cold weather or exposure to another's illness. If your agni is strong, the immune system is supported and much less likely to manifest a problem.

Lovely holidays free of the sugar hangover and illness that is so common are possible. Saying "no thanks" to excess and to foods that are not in your best interest will reward you with great health and peace of mind. There are special, healthy food items to enjoy for your holidays, in moderation. All of the depth of love and richness of holidays will still be available to you.

Dosha Imbalance

- Vata in excess
- Pitta possibly in excess
- Kapha likely in excess

Sections to Reference

- The Process of Eating and Drinking
- Food Combining
- Constipation and Dehydration
- Overeating and Struggles with Weight Control

GUMS, TEETH, AND BAD BREATH

When your digestion is incomplete or disturbed, agni is out of balance and your body creates ama. Urine, feces, and sweat are a normal part of being a healthy human. When these things are not flowing freely due to digestive disturbance, you feel bad in the body and mind. You will notice the effects in the teeth, mouth, gums, breath, and body odor.

Since digestion begins in the mouth, putting strong breath fresheners and chemical toothpaste in the mouth contributes to imbalance in digestion as well. Once the normal flora of the mouth is disturbed, bad breath remains. It calls for more mouthwash and toothpaste to try to fix it or cover it up, perpetuating a vicious cycle.

Previously, in India, cleaning the teeth and gums with a stick from the neem tree was common and effective. There are Ayurvedic toothpastes available that include the bitter and astringent tastes so as not to disturb the balance of the flora in the mouth. Neem is the most common and effective ingredient.

An elderly dentist who had his own naturally beautiful teeth gave me a simple effective preventive practice to prevent tooth decay and gum disease. He said by simply by disturbing the bacteria in the mouth every twelve hours, or twice each day the disease process is not allowed to begin. Do this by the following:

1. Use a tongue scraper to clean the tongue. Note the color and location of any material on the tongue. It tells you a story about where and what kinds of problems are happening in your digestion. Use a metal or bamboo tongue scraper gently from the back of the tongue to front tip to clean it. An accumulation of white (kapha), yellow (pitta), or gray (vata) material indicates ama and weakness in digestion.

One student was able to see that eating prana-filled food in a conscious way helped to keep her tongue in a healthy condition.

Eating food that did not agree with her, poor-quality food, or eating too quickly changed the condition of her tongue immediately, resulting in acne on her face a couple of days later. Become conscious and move beyond the "I will fix it if it breaks" stage in your living.

2. Use a clean, wet toothbrush at a forty-five-degree angle and gently press it under the gum line around the inside and outside of all of your teeth. Rinse your mouth and brush with water thoroughly. Do not brush the gums. Brush on the teeth as needed. Rinse your mouth and brush with water thoroughly. Coating on your teeth is a sign of disturbance in the digestion.
3. Finally, floss between all of the teeth and rinse your mouth thoroughly.

If you feel like you need something else, try two drops of tea tree oil in water and swish through the mouth after your last meal of the day. If you

If you have bleeding gums or find you do at first with this method, keep going. It will stop in a short time, and you will have cleared the accumulation of bacteria out of the gum and root areas that is causing the bleeding. Your teeth and gums will remain in better condition. Swishing sesame oil in your mouth daily for five minutes will also help the condition of the gums and teeth and reduce wrinkles in the face.

This may seem a drastic change from toothpaste with sugar, color, foaming agents, and bacteria killers, but the results are amazing! Allowing the healthy balance of bacteria, fungi, and virus to reestablish itself in your mouth and body will promote health and well-being. In the end, your digestion, teeth, and bank account will benefit greatly.

A simple way to reduce the progression and eliminate the discomfort from receding gums is to gently press your teeth together during elimination. This includes urination and defecation. It will take from one week to one month of regular practice, and you will notice that the tenderness around gums and exposed roots goes away. You may find that you no longer need to use a special toothpaste for exposed roots and receding gums.

Dosha Imbalance

- Vata and Kapha in excess
- Pitta likely also in excess

Sections to Reference

- Digestive Problems
- Constipation and Dehydration
- Principles of Ayurveda

HABITUAL USE OF REFINED SUGAR, SALT, AND PROCESSED FOODS
Refined sugar is one of the more addictive drugs in our society today. It provides instant satisfaction and temporarily controls mental wandering because of its intoxicating effects. Concentrated refined sweets are unhealthy for humans or animals. Studies show that the use of refined sugar causes large fluctuations in the blood sugar of humans and animals. Concentrated sweets are disturbing for the human system. The negative effects are obvious when children eat it and become

hyperactive, agitated, and then sluggish. Adults are just as subject to sugar-induced spikes and crashes; however, most adults are skilled at avoiding the feelings. They counter them with other substances, such as caffeine and medications. Refined sugar is strongly addictive; it creates a significant disconnection between the body and spirit by interfering with the balance of the endocrine system.

Salt in processed form and in excess has a similar effect on the body as refined sugar. Mineral salt or rock salt are less warming than concentrated sea salt or table salt. Cook the salt in your food rather than adding it afterward and moderation is still important.

Daily consumption of refined sugar and excessive salt contributes to imbalance in the lining of the intestines, disturbs agni, and contributes to hormone imbalance, depression, and obesity. Spirit connects to the body through the endocrine system, which produces hormones. When hormones are out of balance, you compromise your connection to the source within you. You might say, "It's not noticeable," but that might be because disconnection is all you know. Living in denial about what is really going on in your body is common. As you work with new attitudes and tools, the denial will fall away.

The dramatic cycles instigated by the consumption of refined sugar and excess salt lead to significant emotional and physical problems. When you are ready to clean up your system, physical and emotional withdrawal may occur. Previously masked feelings come up that you may experience as cravings. You may find yourself substituting one for the other. If what you read in the previous paragraphs annoys you, this can be a sign of attachment. Go without any refined sugar and salt added after cooking for three months or more and see how you feel. Make wise choices in the best interest of your life.

Commitment to being in balance and living life fully will help you avoid addictive substances that harm you. The result is a clarity and inner peace you may not have experienced before. Care enough about yourself to make your own food more often, or ask for special preparations in restaurants.

The first step is to eliminate the refined sugar and processed food from your diet. Eat only fresh sattvic and certain rajasic foods from the section on Ayurvedic Food Classification. Have fresh fruit alone, away from other food by three hours or more. Eat a balance of 60% augmenting and 40% extractive foods. Have a piece of fresh fruit in season if you have cravings.

Dosha Imbalance

- Vata in excess
- Kapha in excess with lethargy and obesity
- Pitta likely in excess

Sections to Reference

- Ayurvedic Food Classification
- Identify Your Dysfunctions: information on addiction
- Blood Sugar Fluctuations
- Appendix A recipes

INTESTINAL GAS AND BELCHING

Many people think it is normal to have large amounts of gas and or belching after eating. Or that it is normal to need to lie down after eating. These situations are not natural with a healthy, balanced meal. The primary cause is imbalanced agni, from eating too frequently, eating too fast, overeating, eating poor-quality food, and eating poor combinations of foods.

Slow the pace of your eating and chew thoroughly to liquid mush, leave four to six hours between meals, and eat only the amount you can hold in your two palms together. When you begin making changes, notice how you feel after each meal and connect it back to what and how you ate.

Likely, the lining of the intestines is compromised, so about one-half cup of aloe juice per day will help restore the balance. Minimize beans and legumes until there has been a significant reduction in the problem. Constipation may contribute to gas and belching as well.

Dosha Imbalance

- Vata in excess
- Pitta possibly in excess
- Kapha often in excess

Sections to Reference

- Ayurvedic Food Classification
- The Process of Eating and Drinking
- Food combining
- Digestive Problems

MOOD FLUCTUATIONS

Drastic mood fluctuations are often the result of too much stimulation, excitement, and expectations. What goes up must come down. For every period of excitement, there's a period of equivalent disappointment. If you keep putting your emphasis on the excitement, you will experience the corresponding lows. You can allow goodness to be present in your life without being attached to the excitement.

Mood fluctuations may also be a result of an overgrowth of yeast in the intestines. This overgrowth can be from constipation, excessive sweets, processed foods, stress, caffeine, or alcohol. When the lining of the intestines is out of balance, hormones become imbalanced, resulting in mood fluctuations. This occurs in both men and women, although it is associated more often with women's menstrual cycle.

In line with the attachments of the mind mentioned above, craving and eating large amounts of hot and spicy foods is a way some people try to keep their moods up, which then results in the corresponding drops.

Restoring the lining of the intestines with sattvic foods in accordance with your constitution is a good place to start. Eliminate the offenders mentioned above. Drink one cup of aloe juice per day. Begin to turn away from the excitement and you will find a peaceful deep joy inside. It takes practice and courage. Be sure to acknowledge your victories to validate your choices. Calmly.

Dosha Imbalance

- Vata in excess
- Pitta sometimes in excess
- Kapha often in excess

Sections to Reference

- Ayurvedic Food Classification
- Conscious Consumption
- Breathing Exercises
- Letting Go of the Illusion of Control

OVEREATING AND STRUGGLES WITH WEIGHT CONTROL

Most overeating is a result of an unconscious attitude and habit formed over time. See the chapter Identifying Your Dysfunctions for additional information. Imbalance in the system drives the habit.

After observing people eating in many different situations, it seems that when people slouch over the table they have unresolved issues in their relationship with food. People who do not slouch appear to have a different attitude. If you find yourself hunching and leaning on the table while you eat, bring your awareness to your posture and stay upright while eating. If you experience some resistance to an upright posture, then allow the feelings to come forth and process them. It is helpful to watch your breathing during the meal. Be sure to pause occasionally and take a relaxed and full breath. You will experience both physical and psychological benefits by making a conscious effort to shift your posture and breathing during mealtime.

Use this very simple tool to help you determine if you are experiencing true hunger or just your mind trying to avoid a feeling and or an emotion. Checking the relative openness of your nostrils will tell you whether your body is still digesting, or fueling agni. At any point during the day, one nostril is blocked more than the other nostril. The right nostril, called *Pingala*, is related to the sun and heat in the body, including your agni. The left nostril, *Ida*, is related to the moon and cooling in the body. If you think you are hungry, check to see which nostril is more open. Close one nostril at a time while breathing through the other. If your hunger for food is real, the right nostril will be more open than the left because the body is no longer digesting the last thing you ate. If the right nostril is closed more than the left, your body is still digesting the last food you ate.

If you have not digested your last meal, do not eat again, no matter what your mind is telling you. If you eat more food on top of partially digested food, you will create a digestive mess, as the correct enzymes are not available for digestion. The result is excess gas, poor-quality digestion of the food, imbalanced agni, and the creation of ama in your system.

Take twelve deep breaths, and drink a half glass of water. Then, see if you are still feeling hungry. If so, allow yourself to acknowledge the feelings and/or the situation you are avoiding. The feelings will pass if you feel them and let them process through; do not become the feeling or act on it. You will not die from it. Just because you experience a feeling does not mean you need do anything about it. Feelings come, and they will go when you allow them to pass. It may not happen in the time frame you think it should. It will definitely happen faster when you let go of the feeling and your expectations of how life "should be."

Feelings are just movements of energy. It requires tremendous energy to stuff these feelings down and avoid them. Moreover, when you stuff your feelings, they do not pass; they are still there. Most often they are not correct. Eating to avoid feeling takes you away from your truth and leads to suffering, obesity, and other serious illness. If the feeling is not true hunger, make a conscious decision not to eat until your system is ready. Ask for help if you feel you cannot do it alone.

In terms of the quantity of food to eat, work with the amount that you can hold in both hands. Yes, you are a Divine design! Fill one-third of the stomach with food, one-third with liquid prior to eating, and leave one-third empty. Some Ayurvedic sources say that one-half, one-quarter, and one-quarter are the proper proportions. I would say the ideal is somewhere between these two perspectives, depending on how it feels to you. The important thing is not to overeat. Drink some liquid, but not too much. The liquid may also be a part of the food you are eating, such as soups and stews. These amounts support optimal digestion, fuel agni, and promote mental clarity. You will learn to recognize what is too much as you become aware of how you feel.

Dosha Imbalance

- Vata in excess
- Kapha in excess
- Pitta possibly in excess

Sections to Reference

- Ayurvedic Food Classification
- Identifying Your Dysfunctions: information on addiction
- The Process of Eating and Drinking

- Habitual Use of Refined Sugar, Salt, and Processed Foods
- Digestive Problems

SLEEP DIFFICULTIES AND ANXIETY

Difficulty sleeping is typically a result of excess stimulation and imbalance in the doshas. This stimulation may be from what you have consumed, including caffeine, refined sugar, and processed foods. Overexertion, overworking, too much computer time, inactivity, movies, or unresolved feelings are also contributors.

Anxiety is a result of attachments to things and the course of events in life. Some people avoid anxious feelings by sleeping excessively. Others are not able to sleep at all. This leads to exhaustion and more aggravation of vata dosha. See the chapter on Identifying Your Dysfunctions for additional information.

A suggestion from Ayurveda for addressing difficulties with sleep is to drink a cup of warm milk with a pinch of nutmeg, cardamom, and cinnamon (the spices vary according to your constitution and balancing needs) and ghee and honey (not in equal portions) just before bed. If you have excess pitta (fire) in your system, use maple syrup instead of honey. In my experience, this promotes peaceful sleep and helps reduce anxiety.

Additionally, eat warm, cooked foods rather than raw, and opt for preparations that include oil rather than those that are dry. Gently rub sesame oil into the bottoms of the feet and top of the head just as you get into bed. It will assist the calming of vata and sooth the path to peaceful sleep and reduce anxiety. Do not perform a vigorous foot massage as it will stimulate your system. Wear socks to keep the oil off your sheets.

Dosha Imbalance

- Vata in excess
- Pitta and kapha in excess, possibly

Sections to Reference

- Principles of Ayurveda
- Ayurvedic Food Classification
- Digestive Problems
- Appendix A, kitchadi recipes

STIFF AND ACHING JOINTS

Avoid or minimize the nightshade family if you have any joint problems, as they may aggravate the stiffness. This includes potatoes, tomatoes, eggplant, and bell peppers. Try eliminating them for three weeks at least and see how you feel.

Joint discomfort may also result from excessive internal dryness. This means vata is in excess and has left its natural home in the colon. Give yourself an application of oil each day. There are Ayurvedic oils with herbs decocted into them to help with excess vata in the joints. Using raw sesame oil or the appropriate oil for your constitution is a good place to start. Be sure to apply the oil to the joints with the palm of your hand and rub the oil in as if you are feeding the joints. Begin with the sacrum and work down each of the legs and feet. Move to the remainder of the torso, the arms and hands, and the neck and head. Leave the oil on at least twenty minutes before bathing with warm water and without soap; even five minutes will make a difference. This will help to rehydrate the joints and skin. The cause of the stiffness and aching is ama in the system, most often from poor food quality, poor food combining, and poor eating habits such as overeating and eating too fast.

Dosha Imbalance

- Vata in excess
- Pitta in excess, possibly

Sections to Reference

- Ayurvedic Food Classification
- The Process of Eating and Drinking
- Food Combining
- Digestive Problems
- Constipation and Dehydration

Discover Harmony and Balance

TRANSITIONING FROM THE OLD WAYS

*R*estoring your connection to your innermost self and practicing new behaviors on an ongoing basis are the keys to recovery from poor eating and drinking habits. Your energy will shift as soon as you make the decision to open your mind and heart toward the discovery of your higher self. Subtle changes in your thoughts will shift your awareness. Working with these shifts in awareness will transform your thinking. Like attracts like; the more you focus on higher vibration activities related to consumption, the more you will attract that vibration.

Become willing to revise some traditions and to let go of others. Walk yourself through the details of a week: pick out the activities and rituals you are willing to let go of and then do so. Develop and practice new rituals that speak to your truth and open a new path for you.

Be willing to do things differently at the holidays. Make clear, conscious choices about being with others who support your changes. Invite friends and family who seem rigid in their old ways to try something new. You may be surprised. A workable solution to any situation, without compromising your own health and well-being, is available. A quote from an Ayurvedic text addresses this simply in saying, "The inner intelligence of the body is the ultimate and supreme genius. It mirrors the wisdom of the universe."

There are so many techniques and approaches to working with your health, the body, and well-being. Many of them are valid and can be helpful. Moderation is the key. A gentle variety of foods suited to your constitution will help you find harmony in living. Keep it simple for yourself and be aware of the results.

The following will assist you in healing during your change to healthful living:

- Clean out toxins by eating with gently cleansing foods. Practice one day of kitchadi each week See Appendix A for kitchadi cleansing recipes.
- Consume foods with plenty of prana. You will take a step up in energy and vitality.
- Eat your main meal at midday if possible, then a lighter meal early in the evening. Do not eat within two hours of sleep or sexual activity.
- Addictions are blocks to healing; acknowledge and turn away from them to clear your path.
- Clean up your relationships to clear the path for more fulfilled living.
- If you experience pain, you are in resistance. Let go.
- Practice devotional fasting one day each month if you feel balanced and ready to do so. Keep your Divine source in mind throughout the day. Using a mantra or contemplative affirmation is helpful.

- Healing happens when you go deeply inside and clean out the old. This will help shave off the sharp, rigid edges of ego and allow life to unfold, moment by moment.

BLESSINGS FOR MEALS—SOFTEN YOUR HEART WITH GRATITUDE

Bring the sacred nature into your eating by taking a moment before each meal to be grateful and present. This is a major component of conscious eating. The following blessings are from various traditions around the world. Some are thousands of years old; some are more recent. Prayer is your most powerful expression of intention. Choose one or more to work with regularly at your mealtime. You can create your own prayers too.

The food is Brahma (creative energy)
Its essence is Vishnu (preserving energy)
The eater is Shiva (destructive energy)
No sickness due to food can come
To one who eats with this knowledge.
                (Sanskrit blessing)

Bless these Thy gifts, most gracious God,
From whom all goodness springs
Make clean our hearts and feed our souls
With good and joyful things.
             (Traditional Christian grace)

And when you crush an apple with your teeth, say to it in your heart,
"Your seeds shall live in my body,

And the buds of your tomorrow shall blossom in my heart,
And your fragrance shall be my breath,
And together we shall rejoice through all the seasons."
(Khalil Gibran, The Prophet)

Dear Father and Divine Mother, givers of life
The food that lies before us we humbly offer to you,
Source and creator of all things.
We pray that in love, faith and truth we may use these simple fruits of the soil
to better serve you, all beings and
to nourish the rising flame, our souls within.
(Unknown)

Let us give thanks for the food we are about to eat.
May there be food for all, abundant and healthful.
Let us have the wisdom to choose to eat only food that enhances our precious energy and sustains us through our labors and rest.
(Adapted from An Haggadah of Liberation)

May we walk with grace and may the light of the universe shine upon our path.
(Anonymous)

In this plate of food, I see the entire universe supporting my existence.
(Thich Nhat Hanh)

From food, all creatures are produced, and all creatures that dwell on earth, by food, they live and into food, they finally pass.

Food is the chief among beings. He obtains all food who worships the Divine as food.

(Taittiriya Upanishad)

Let us live happily, though we call nothing our own.
Let us be like God, feeding on love.

(the Dhammapada)

Let us be together; let us eat together.
Let us be vital together; let us be radiating truth, radiating the light of life.
Never shall we denounce anyone, nor entertain negativity.

(the Upanishads)

May we all grow in grace and peace and not neglect the silence printed in the center of our being. It will not fail us.

(Thomas Merton)

Make a silent prayer acknowledging yourself as a vehicle of light, giving thanks for all that has come today.

(Dhyani Ywahoo)

What is well planted cannot be uprooted...Cultivate virtue in your own person and it becomes part of you. Cultivate it in the family and it will abide. Cultivate it in the community and it will live and grow. Cultivate it in the state and it will flourish abundantly. Cultivate it in the world and it will become universal.

> (Tao Te Ching)

Oh, Supreme Being, Lord of the Universe
This food is an offering to you in absolute gratitude and love.
I take it in freely, receiving the prana, wonder and nurturing,
So that I may give back to you, and all beings.
Thy will be done. Om Shanti.

> (Anonymous)

BREATHING EXERCISES—RELEASE THE OLD AND BRING IN THE NEW

The word prana refers to life force and to the breath. Your breath is the source of your life force. You can access places deep within the psyche with the use of your breath. When you go into fear, often your first response is to hold the breath. As you connect to your source within, energetic channels open up and allow more energy to flow. As the energy flows, you release fear. Learning to work with your breath is a large part of living consciously in connection with your spirit.

The word *pranayama* literally means breath control. The practices of pranayama are a powerful and profound method of retraining the mind to focus, and an integral part of Yoga. These practices teach you to channel your energy in and around your body at your will. Pranayama practices are cleansing, creating heat in the body to remove blockages. Performed correctly with specific detail, they render a powerful effect. They are cumulative practices that grow with you as you go deeper. Practiced incorrectly, they can be harmful. Therefore, they are beyond the scope of this book. I recommend that you learn pranayama from a qualified teacher. Go to halepule.com for more information.

You can start some simple but challenging breathing exercises that do not require an experienced teacher. They will help you strengthen your mind and connect to your authentic self.

Learning to observe and count the breaths is a good place to start. Sit with the spine upright. (Lie down if sitting is too difficult.) Close your eyes.

Count your breaths and you will begin to focus. Each inhale and exhale is one round. The breath should remain comfortable and not stressful. Be sure to keep the entire tongue relaxed and off of the roof of the mouth. Next, begin to count the length of each inhale and each exhale. Practice slowing down each inhale and exhale. Bring them to the same length and sound. If you feel anxious or tense then make the exhale twice as long as the inhale. The inhale and exhale may be three or four counts each or they may be more. Begin by practicing for three minutes then increase to five minutes. Set a timer. If three minutes feels like too much, start with one or two minutes. Commit to something and go with it for at least one week and see how you feel. Be interested in your breath and the miracle that it creates. Your body cannot function without it.

Each time the mind wanders off, gently bring it back to your breath. This will happen and this is the practice, gently bringing the mind back.

If you are feeling anxious or irritated, exhale twice as long as the inhale. As you begin to feel calmer in the practice, switch again and work with even inhale and exhale. As you are finishing, switch back to exhaling twice as long to relax.

Stay flexible in your work with the breath. The mind attaches to familiarity. Challenging the mind is a good thing. The ego, which prefers external focus, will tell you to stop because working with the breath draws your focus inward.

You should not feel pressure in the head or excessive stress during or after working with the breath. If you do, you are pushing or trying too hard. This is counterproductive.

Be sure to stay awake. If you go to sleep, that is what you are practicing, and you already know how to do that. Remember, what you practice is what you get. The purpose is to learn to focus your mind by watching your breath. If you find you are going to sleep, keep the eyes half open in a soft gaze at one spot, something that is not moving.

A second exercise is to begin with the inhale and exhale as suggested above, adding a one-count pause after the inhale. Next, add a one-count pause after the exhale, so that you are pausing after each inhale and exhale. Use your mind to pause the breath, not tensing your body. Do it from the inside. Be calm, slow, and focused. If you begin to feel anxious or stressed, eliminate the pause. Go back to working with a continuous inhale and exhale. Work with a timer, beginning with one to five minutes. You can increase the time gradually as long as there is no tension or ill effects.

A third exercise adds a slight constriction of the throat to the inhale and exhale process. By closing the throat slightly, make a sound with your breath. It comes from the throat, not the nose, and sounds a bit like the hum of a fan. This subtle roar on both the inhale and the exhale requires your focus. After working with the sound for one to three minutes, switch to a quiet subtle breath with as little sound as possible on both the inhale and the exhale. Continue this practice for one to three minutes.

With these exercises, you can also count a particular number of breaths instead of using a timer. Establish the number before you begin. If the number you choose feels stressful, adjust to a lesser amount.

You can do these exercises free of counting or timers, but in the beginning the mind will need some training to stay with it. You can pause anytime during your day and focus on the breath for just a few moments using any of these techniques.

MEDITATIONS—LEARN TO FOCUS AND MANAGE YOUR ENERGY

Meditation takes you beyond your perceptions to a place where your consciousness, subconscious, and unconscious come together. It takes you to the depths of your awareness and to the unknown. The first steps are willingness and courage. Five minutes per day is enough to get started. Even a one-minute conscious pause will make a difference. Beginning with the simplest form of meditation can establish discipline, which focuses the mind and frees your spirit.

You may choose to focus and concentrate on a mantra or a particular prayer, driving those sacred words deeply into your consciousness, or you may use the steps described below. There are many methods to get started. Choose one and stick with it. It should not be a mechanical practice, but it will be on the surface initially. If the mind becomes agitated, remember it is just the ego. Rise above this self-centered will and learn the right use of your will. You are retraining your mind and nervous system. Your thoughts and desires will come within your control.

As you continue your practice, it will grow deeper. The insights you gain will translate into your daily living and cultivate connectedness. Learn to be the witness of your life by watching your own consciousness at all times. This requires ongoing practice. As you continue to use your awareness, it will take you beyond time and space. Remember, you are that which you seek.

To begin your meditation, sit with the spine upright. Imagine a string from the top of your head pulling your spine up to the sky. Roll your shoulders back and relax them down. You may need to sit on a pillow, at the wall, or in a chair. If you need to lie down to begin, do so.

The purpose of these meditations is to raise your consciousness and help you connect to your deepest truth. Be sure to stay awake. Although there is a great deal of activity going on in your sleep, these meditations are most helpful when done first in the waking state.

Initially, you may like to record your voice and play the meditations to yourself. Eventually, you will be able to practice them on your own.

Your mind is going to wander and wonder. That is what it knows how to do. When it does wander, as soon as you recognize it, *gently* bring it back. This is the process. Criticizing and chastising yourself feeds your ego. It does not help you or anyone else. The ego will fight this process. This is not about being right or doing it perfectly. Let it go. Remember, life is a process, as is meditation. You are taking time to connect to your deepest self, your Divine source.

MEDITATION FOR CLEARING YOUR ENERGY
This takes a matter of seconds, with eyes open or closed. Learn to find the center of your head by drawing a line between the

eyebrows straight back and from the tops of the ears straight across. Where the two lines cross is the center of your head. Connect the center of your head to your crown with a white line of energy. This enables you to utilize your knowingness from the crown chakra. Set your energy like this daily. Place your attention in the center of your head. Imagine an energetic cord, as large as you like, going from the base of your spine down to the center of the planet. Allow this cord to be as large as you like. Be specific and clear. Imagine hooking it in and turning it on release to let go of anything that is not you. Let go of "should," "supposed to," and any voices or considerations that are not your own. Feel yourself grounded and let go of anything that is not you. Allow the planet to strengthen you and help you find your center and truth in this moment. Follow this with the meditation for replenishing.

MEDITATION FOR REPLENISHING

Replenish yourself and fill up any space resulting from letting go of something. Imagine a big gold sun over your head. Fill that gold sun with what you would like to replenish yourself with, self-love, love of the Divine, playfulness, clarity, joy, and freedom. When you are ready, pop a hole in your gold sun. Let bright gold, high-vibration energy pour in through the top of your head. Let it fill up all of the cells of your body, fill up your grounding cord, and fill up the energetic bubble around your body, about one half meter on all sides. Continue to allow the gold energy to pour in until you feel completely filled up, particularly in the areas where you have let go of something. Enjoy the replenished feeling. If you do not see anything, it is okay. Imagine that you can. Sit in silence for a few moments, twenty minutes, or an hour as you like.

MORNING AND EVENING MEDITATIONS

The practice of contemplation, or full, deep consideration, is a useful approach to beginning a meditation practice. Select a verse or a point of focus and sit with it for the time frame you select. For example, in the morning sit facing east. Contemplate the sun and all of the wonders it brings to you, such as warmth, light, energy, and transformation. See it rising in your mind's eye. Acknowledge the connection between you and the universe. Take three deep breaths and sit with whatever comes up. Let everything come and go freely. The feelings stay and become stagnant when you hold on. Let go into the sunrise. When you are complete, open your eyes into the light and enjoy your day.

At sunset, sit facing west. Place your focus on gratitude for the sun and for darkness. Acknowledge all that night brings to you, including rest and rejuvenation. Contemplate your day, releasing any residual feelings and emotions. Realize your connection to the universe. Let go into the sunset. Enjoy this moment.

The practice of agnihotra, a Vedic fire ceremony is a great healing and opportunity for meditation and connection to all that it. See www.halepule.com/agnihotra for more information.

If it feels too difficult, choose a particular verse or prayer that stimulates devotion and gratitude in you. For example, if you are working on releasing perfectionism, then repeat "I am a child of God, I am enough" or "All is well, my Divine source is present." Select an acknowledgement of your source that touches your heart. Use that same one for an indefinite time. In other words, stick with it. If your mind is racing, focus on twelve deep breaths and go back to the verse or prayer.

MEDITATION FOR CLEARING BLOCKAGES AND CREATING WELLNESS

Sit in a meditative position described previously. Breathe evenly, being aware of your complete inhale, exhale, and the transition between them. Clear your energy and replenish yourself, as mentioned above. Now, bring your awareness to the cells in your body. If you prefer, you can imagine your body on a screen in front of you. See all of the individual cells and their interiors. Notice how they are vibrating and moving. Notice the places that seem stagnant or stuck. Again, if you do not see anything, just imagine you do and work from there. Imagine a cosmic paintbrush that has an endless supply of cobalt blue healing paint coming from it. Use this cosmic paintbrush to bathe every cell of your body, on the inside and outside, with the cobalt blue energy. Imagine the cobalt blue stimulating the digestion of nutrients within each cell of the body. Focus on the areas of challenge, such as the stomach or intestines, for improving digestion. Focus on the sinuses and the digestive tract for healing from allergies. Notice if you carry a belief that this is not possible. When you are ready, allow the cosmic paintbrush to bathe the area where the belief resides, freeing it up. Let go of the belief and the need to "know." Completely bathe the heart center, around the center of the chest, two centimeters to the left and two centimeters to the right, then include the upper back. Breathe in and out in this area until you feel free. When you feel complete with the healing cobalt blue energy, replenish yourself with a big gold sun as described above. Give special attention to filling up the areas where you let go of something or felt stuck. Be in deep appreciation.

Mantra meditation

Traditionally, a mantra is a name or verse representing God, or your source, that you repeat to help your mind focus. A teacher may give it to you, or you can select your own. A mantra can also be a verse or prayer that has a devotional meaning for you. Your mantra can be in Sanskrit or your own language that helps you connect to the feeling of your source. For example, you might select the Om (universal consciousness), the Lord's Prayer, Rama, Allah, the Gayatri Mantra, the St. Francis Prayer, or another.

Use a string of mala beads to help you count 108 repetitions. Repeating the mantra 108 times is auspicious. Work with the mantra a minimum of three times in each session and all day long as you can. You can also count on your fingers or just repeat the mantra in your sitting for a period of time you select. These are just techniques. It's most important that you are attracted to the mantra and allow it to touch you deeply cultivating connection. Be willing to use it at any time in your life, not just in your meditation time. Your mantra will calm your emotions and make that energy available to you. If something makes you anxious or angry, go for a walk and repeat your mantra until you can refocus your mind. The anxiety and anger will dissipate, your insides will slow down, and you will feel better. This is an empowering step to take charge of your mind.

Five elements meditation

Sitting with the spine upright or lying down with the spine straight as you need, close the eyes, take three deep breaths to focus your attention, and relax the body. Feel the earth beneath your body. Feel the buttocks, legs, and feet. If you are lying down, feel the back of your head, arms, legs, and your entire back connecting with the floor and the earth. Notice the movement of your prana in your body. Imagine the movement of prana flowing freely between the earth and your body. Let all resistance and tension melt away. See it dissolving. Enjoy the free flow of prana with the earth.

Next, imagine the movement of prana as fluids in your body. Feel the moisture in the mouth, eyes, nose, and genitals. Notice the flow in and out of the heart as it beats and the flow through the veins and arteries. Connect to each of the organs floating inside your body. See yourself in this body as part of the vast ocean of consciousness. Enjoy this place of fluid movement.

Now be aware of the processing of all that you have consumed. See the process of digestion of food, sounds, sights, smells, emotions, and anything else. Allow your awareness in digestion to transform these things to pure consciousness. Release any resistance and let go of toxins on all levels. Observe and be a witness to this process.

Next, feel the movement of prana as breath and life force moving through the body as you breathe. Fill the lungs slowly and empty them slowly and completely. Notice the downward movement of the diaphragm with the inhale, and expand the chest completely. Release all tension and toxins with the exhale. Experience your body and energy field about one half meter around the body. See and feel it as whole, closing up any holes. Sit in the awareness of your energy and breath.

Now be aware of your attention in the center of your head. Then step into pure consciousness by taking your attention just above the head and looking down at the body. Observe your body from this point of view. Realize that part of you is still safely in the body. Experience you consciousness from here. When you are ready, bring your attention back into the center of your head. Be aware of your energy filling the entire body, fully to the fingertips, toes, tip of the nose, and the bubble about eighteen inches around you.

Again, practice awareness of you, in your body. Take three deep conscious breaths, open your eyes, and experience the new you.

OTHER PRACTICES FROM YOGA AND AYURVEDA

The steps and practices discussed in this book come from Yoga and Ayurveda. I have put them in simple terms for your use. The book *Yoga for Your Type* by Sandra Summerfield Kozak and David Frawley is a very useful tool for working with the doshas and asana (posture) practice. If you already have an asana practice, you can incorporate these principles into that practice. If you go to asana classes, acknowledge your Divine source throughout the class. Allow time for your savasana (relaxation pose) at the end of practice or class. Relaxing, even when your mind wants to go eat, will help strengthen your will and prevent unhealthy eating.

The practice of Agnihotra, an ancient fire ceremony, purifies and cleanses the atmosphere. It has its origin in the Vedas from which Ayurveda is drawn. Veda means "pure knowledge" and is an ancient treasure house of information. Given at the time of creation for all of humanity, this knowledge is universal.

Agnihotra balances the cycle of nature and nourishes human life. In my experience, Agnihotra reduces stress, leads to greater clarity of thought, improves overall health, increases energy, and leaves the mind full of love. Many people have experienced that it renews brain cells, revitalizes the skin, purifies the blood, cleanses the negative effects of pollution, and is a holistic approach to life. The agnihotra practice and ash are used in organic farming and other therapies. See halepule.com for additional information.

Enliven all of your life with an attitude of connectedness, and you will discover a life beyond your dreams.

Summary

Let's review some general guidelines for eating and drinking:

- Eat on a regular schedule with the heavier meal midday if possible. If you do not feel hungry at mealtime, wait to eat until the next mealtime. Do not compensate by eating more than normal.
- Bath before eating if possible or at a minimum wash your hands. After eating, wash the hands, eyes and mouth.
- Eat slowly. Enjoy your food through all of your five senses. Work on chewing to liquid mush, remembering that digestion begins in the mouth.
- Eat a maximum of four items at one meal. Do not snack while cooking or between meals.
- Eat only as much as would fit in your two hands in one sitting.
- Drink water twenty minutes before eating to reinforce hydration; drink about half a cup with the meal, only if you like. If you are thirsty in your meal, then you may be dehydrated. Consider filling your stomach halfway, leaving one quarter for fluid and one quarter for gases. Learn what this is for you and your body, rather than what your mind may think.
- Eat in a peaceful atmosphere and with a peace-filled attitude. Enjoy the food and eat in silence or with light, simple conversation. Save complicated matters for another time.
- Pray and show reverence before each meal. The meal is a sacred gift from the universe. Express an attitude of

appreciation and eat only what you need. Offer the food to your source or God before eating in order to purify it and to remove negativity trapped in it.

- Realize that everything you do is "eating." Everything you experience digests in your consciousness.
- Engage in activities that support goodness and purity. Just as "you are what you eat," you are what you do.

Live lightly on the earth. Become aware of the natural resources around you and those you use. Reduce, reuse, rethink, and recycle. Make it a project with family and friends to identify waste in all areas of your life. Eliminate unnecessary usage and waste. If it feels uncomfortable and silly, laugh at yourself and keep going. After all, look at the results the old ways brought you. Owning many things, throwing away many things, and excess food do not make you happier. It causes confusion and delusion. Make conscious choices, and you will realize the interconnectedness in all of life. Realize the cause and effect in your living.

Learn to understand and appreciate the rhythms and relationships in nature and your part in it. Consider the life of a plant—from seed to fruit and back to the earth again. Consider the life of a human or other animal—from conception to death and back to the earth and ethers again.

Use the tools in this book to find peace in nature and within you. Take care of your body for internal strength and happiness. Select and prepare food with love and gratitude. Not just on holidays or special times, but all of the time. It will make your life more interesting. Practice replacing judgment with laughter. Realize that as you are healing your body and soul, you are healing your community and the earth. Explore your imagination and higher self through meditation, prayer, journaling, and quiet time alone just sitting. Practice *being*.

Pause, you are here. You are in a new place of faith, courage, and openness. Embracing the change will give you the strength to stay on the path through the challenging times. You have the power to change your mind. Change your attitude about food, eating, and consumption, and your heart will open.

Acceptance of reality and your starting point will free you to move forward. Be willing to make changes gradually and results will come. Be aware of the details and synchronicities in your life. They will assist you in staying balanced and moving forward. You will become present, steadier in your actions, and more joyful in your life. Remember that resisting change creates suffering. Follow the ebb and flow and your life will transform you to see your true self.

These are tools for living consciously. The point is to choose something to work with and stick with it. Practice what you want and keep going in that direction. If you get off track, pick up where you left off and move forward again. Commit to your own well-being by drawing on the infinite source of power within. Go beyond the intellect. Go with your deepest truth and soar.

Appendix A _ Recipes

Recipes are a guideline and not a rigid set of rules. There are no report cards for performance. Be present and loving when you cook. Enjoy your cooking and eating at a moderate pace. Let them be a prayer and a gift of love. Slow down and be attentive with all of your spirit. Put your love, gratitude, and tenderness into the food and great things will come from whatever you prepare.

Each time I cook, it is a new creation. All previous experience is a part of this new creation. Many books and friends are a part of the inspiration from which these recipes evolved. Each experience in the kitchen is a new adventure. Here are some suggestions for your meals. Consider these recipes as a starting point for your adventures. The intention is to offer primarily sattvic food for balance and harmony. You may need to alter some of the recipes for the optimal balance of your doshas at a particular point in time. There are unlimited possibilities. Assume that in all of the recipes, ingredients are suggested to be all organically (cleanly) grown with as much fresh and local produce as possible.

Breakfast Grains (serves 2)
Preparation time: 30 minutes or less, mostly unattended
  1 cup pearl barley (basmati rice, quinoa, or millet are also nice
  choices depending on your dosha)
  ½ teaspoon cinnamon
  ½ teaspoon cumin
  ½ teaspoon coriander
  ½ teaspoon ginger
  1 handful raisins (optional)
  1 tablespoon ghee
  2 cups water

Soak grains overnight. Add spices and ghee and bring to a boil. Simmer until tender but chewy. A pressure cooker eliminates the need for soaking and the grains will cook in 15 minutes or less. Add a little extra water with the pressure cooker and particularly if you like a soupy consistency. Be simple and creative. Change the spices to just ground cardamom and a pinch of rock salt for another variation.

Fruit breakfast (serves 2)
Preparation time: less than 5 minutes
    2 pieces fresh ripe fruit such as apples, pears or whatever is in season.
    1 Tbsp ghee or coconut oil
    A few mint leaves
    A small squeeze of lime juice
    Herbal tea and/or water

Cut the fruit into bite size pieces and simmer gently for 1-3 minutes in ghee or coconut oil (in warm weather) with the mint. Add the lime juice while cooking.

Roots and Greens (serves 4)
Preparation time: 15 minutes or less
 1 large bunch of kale or collard greens or a mixture of the two
 3 large carrots or 2 medium beets
 2 tablespoons ghee (coconut oil or olive oil)
 ½ teaspoon cumin seeds
 ½ teaspoon turmeric
 ½ teaspoon coriander
 ⅛ teaspoon asafoetida (hing)
 1 tablespoons hijiki
 ½–1 cup water

Wash greens well and chop or tear by hand into half-inch slices or smaller. Grate the carrots into a bowl. Bring ghee to a simmer in a medium to large pan with lid. Then add spices, hijiki, and simmer until the seeds pop and the aroma is present. Add the chopped greens and simmer with closed lid for 3–5 minutes, stirring once. Then add water and the grated carrot and simmer for 5–8 minutes until soft. Turn off the heat and let sit with lid on for 3–5 minutes then serve.

Simple Soup (serves 2)
Preparation time: 15 minutes
   ½ cup white basmati rice
   6 cups water
   2 cups chopped veggies (such as zucchini and broccoli or sweet
   potato and asparagus)
   1 teaspoon barley miso
   ½ teaspoon dried basil
   ½ teaspoon coriander
   ½ teaspoon freshly grated ginger
   ½ teaspoon turmeric
   Chopped parsley or green shiso for garnish

Bring water and rice to a boil with the spices. Reduce heat to simmer, add vegetables and cover 5–10 minutes or until the veggies change color. Remove from heat and add miso. Let sit for 5 minutes more. Garnish with parsley or green shiso.

Roll Up (serves one)
Preparation time: less than 5 minutes
  1 sprouted grain chapatti/tortilla
  ½ cup clover or sprouted sunflower sprouts
  Grated or chopped veggies (carrot, beet, asparagus, cucumber, etc.)
  1 teaspoon stone ground mustard
  1 teaspoon flax meal

Warm chapatti on a flame or in an oven until soft, one minute or less. Add ingredients and roll up. Add rice or dhal from your previous meal to the roll up as well. A pinch of black pepper or powdered cumin and coriander is also nice to aid digestion. Be careful not to add to many different vegetables. Be creative and find two to work with in accordance with balancing your dosha. Eat it alone or with a cup of plain miso soup.

Spring Vegetables (serves 4)
Preparation time: 20 minutes
 15-20 stalks asparagus
 2 cups chopped pumpkin or squash of your choice
 2 tablespoons ghee (or coconut, sesame, sunflower oil)
 ½ teaspoon mustard seeds
 ½ teaspoon cumin
 ½ teaspoon coriander
 ½ teaspoon grated fresh ginger

Chop vegetables into medium-sized pieces. In a wok or large sauce-pan, heat ghee and add spices. Cook until the seeds start popping. Add the squash and stir to coat with ghee and spices. Add enough water to submerge the squash about one third and lightly cook until beginning to soften. Add the asparagus and cook for an additional 5 minutes with the lid on. Serve with a whole grain, any legume or the dhal in the next recipe.

Traditional Dhal (serves 4)
Preparation time: 30 minutes or less
  ½ cup split mung beans
  2 tablespoons shredded coconut (optional)
  2 tablespoons ghee
  ½ teaspoon cumin seeds
  1 teaspoon grated ginger
  2 cups water
  ½ teaspoon powder turmeric
  Pinch of asafoetida
  1 teaspoon coriander powder
  ½ teaspoon rock salt

Wash split mung beans until water runs clear. Heat pan and dry roast split mung beans with coconut, spices and ghee until the aroma is notable. Heat the water and add to beans. Cover and simmer over medium heat for 30–40 minutes (15–20 minutes with a pressure cooker). Serve with basmati rice, quinoa, or barley.

Another Dhal Variation (serves 4)
Preparation time: 30–40 minutes or less
    1 cup split mung beans
    3 cups warm water
    1 tablespoon ghee
    Pinch of minced chili pepper
    ½ teaspoon grated ginger
    ½ teaspoon cumin seeds
    ¼ teaspoon turmeric
    ½ teaspoon rock salt
    1 teaspoon coriander powder
    ¼ teaspoon asafoetida
    ½ teaspoon fresh lime juice

Wash split mung beans until water runs clear. Place in pan and add warm water. Cover and simmer over medium heat for 30–40 minutes. Heat the ghee in a small pan. Brown the chili pepper, ginger, and cumin seeds in ghee for a few minutes. Add the remaining spices (except the lime juice) toward the end of the browning. Add to beans with lime juice and remaining water as desired. Cover and continue to simmer for an additional 10 minutes over low heat. Add additional water to thin the dhal making it easier to digest.

Rice and Dhal Combo (serves 4)

Preparation time: 45 minutes mostly unattended; about 20 minutes with a pressure cooker

    1 cup brown basmati rice

    ½ cup split mung beans

    2 tablespoons ghee

    ¼ teaspoon asafoetida

    ½ teaspoon cumin seeds

    1–2 tablespoons shredded coconut

    2 strips kombu, cut into small pieces

    3 ½–4 cups warm water

    ½ teaspoon ginger

    ½ teaspoon coriander

    ½ teaspoon turmeric

Use your hand to wash rice and split mung beans until water runs clear. Place in pot and turn on heat. Stir in ghee, asafoetida, and cumin seeds, coating all of the rice and beans. Add coconut and kombu. Stir and simmer for another minute or two. Add ginger, coriander, turmeric, and warm water and stir. Cook mostly covered on a regular stove or put in pressure cooker for 15–20 minutes (add ½–1 cup more water with a pressure cooker).

Greens (serves 4)
Preparation time: 15 minutes
  1 large bunch kale or collards
  1 cup water
  ½ teaspoon fresh grated ginger
  2 tablespoons olive oil (or sunflower oil, coconut oil, almond oil)
  Juice from ¼ lime

Wash and chop greens into small strips. Warm the oil in a saucepan then add spices and simmer until the aroma comes up. Stir in the greens and simmer until tender. Stir in mint, turn off heat and let sit for 5 minutes.

Hummus (serves 8)
Preparation time: 2 hours, mostly unattended (not including soaking time)

2 cups garbanzo beans (or 1 cup garbanzo and 1 cup adzuki)
½ teaspoon asafoetida
3 strips kombu, cut into small pieces
3 tablespoons olive oil (sesame or sunflower oil)
3 tablespoons tahini
Juice from ½ lemon or lime
½ teaspoon black pepper
½ cup chopped cilantro or green shiso (optional)
Water

Soak beans 6-12 hours. Be sure to add water twice the depth of the beans to allow for their expansion. Drain the beans. Warm the oil in the pot, add spices and kombu, simmering until the aroma comes up. Add the beans and stir. Then add water to cover the top of the beans. Bring to boil and reduce the heat to simmer with the cover on. Let simmer about two hours until soft (a pressure cooker will reduce cooking time to 20-25 minutes). Stir them periodically and add water as needed. Let cool before blending with the liquid from the cooking pot. Add olive oil, tahini, black pepper, and lime or lemon. Add additional liquid as necessary to achieve your desired thickness. Serve as is or garnish with cilantro or green shiso.

Guacamole (serves 2)
Preparation time: 5 minutes
    2 small avocados, peeled and pitted
    ⅛ teaspoon cayenne pepper
    Pinch of rock salt
    1 cup chopped cilantro
    Juice of ½ small lime or lemon

Place all ingredients in blender or in bowl mixing until smooth.

Ghee

Ghee is an ancient and sattvic food. Ideal for cooking, it does not burn unless heated excessively. It blends with the food nutrients and nourishes the body, supporting agni. Ghee is good for all doshas in moderation and minimal use for kapha imbalance. Do not use salted or commercial butter when making ghee, as the salt and contaminants become more concentrated in the ghee.

Although you can find ghee at your local store, you might find it more rewarding and less expensive to make at home. Use it as you would normally use butter. The taste may seem unusual at first—maybe a distant cousin of butter. Your palate quickly adjusts, and soon you forget why you ever found butter interesting!

To make ghee, place one pound organic unsalted butter in a stainless steel, glass or cast iron saucepan (not non-stick or aluminum). Melt the butter and bring to a simmer. It will pop and speak to you. Say a blessing of gratitude over it. Be aware of all of the people and the cow who has brought this to you. Let it simmer uncovered and stay in the area to watch it and enjoy the aroma, color and sound. Once the ghee is simmering, do not touch it – let it be! It will be about 15 minutes for one pound, but the length of time, as well as the color and amount of foam, varies according to the food the cows ate, the season of the year, your pot, your stove and current weather conditions. The process is somewhat unique each time. The ghee is ready when the popping stops. Foam may form on the top and some black skim on the bottom of the pan. As it stops popping remove it from the heat immediately or it will burn. Allow it to cool for about 15 minutes. Strain through a fine stainless steel colander or unbleached cheesecloth into a clean, dry jar that tolerates heat. Place the jar in a large bowl to catch any ghee that misses the jar. Store the ghee in the cupboard, not the refrigerator. It becomes better with age.

Split Pea Soup (serves 4)
Preparation time: 1½ hours, mostly unattended
  1 cup split peas
  1 cup quinoa
  2 strips of kombu, cut into small pieces
  ½ teaspoon cumin powder
  ½ teaspoon coriander powder
  ¾ teaspoon ginger powder
  ¾ teaspoon turmeric
  1–3 tablespoons ghee
  4 cups water
  ½ cup chopped basil

Soak split peas for 1 to 2 hours. Pour off water. Thoroughly rinse quinoa and place in a pot or saucepan with split peas. Add kombu and spices and ghee to pot and stir for 2–3 minutes over medium heat. Add water and bring to a boil. Simmer while covered until the peas are tender, about 45 minutes. Stir a few times during the cooking process. Add water as needed to maintain your preferred consistency. In a pressure cooker, this soup is ready in 25 minutes without soaking. Enjoy it in the cooler seasons.

Pesto (serves 4)
Preparation time: 10 minutes
    4 cups washed and chopped fresh spinach and fresh basil
    ½ cup olive oil
    ½ cup water (more if desired)
    ½ cup fresh paneer or tofu (optional)
    Pinch of black pepper
    Pinch of rock salt
    One handful pine nuts or peeled almonds (optional)

Simmer the spices and nuts in the oil until the aroma is present. Place all ingredients in the blender and puree. Add more water or olive oil as needed for consistency. Depending on the strength of your blender, you may need to blend, stop and stir, and then return to blending until mixture is smooth. Use pesto on cooked whole grains, pizza or cooked vegetables.

Pizza (serves 2–3)
Preparation time: 40 minutes
    Crust
    2 cups whole wheat flour or a mixture of whole wheat and rice
    or barley
    ½ teaspoon ground rock salt
    ¼ cup sunflower or olive oil
    ½ - 1 cup water

Preheat oven to 400F. Combine dry ingredients in a mixing bowl stirring with your clean hands. Add oil and then water as needed to form a ball of soft dough. Turn the dough out onto a floured cutting board and knead it gently 5–10 times. Lightly oil a stainless steel or glass pan and press dough into the pan, making an edge up the sides with your fingers. Bake for 6 to 10. Reduce temperature in oven to 375F for final cooking.

Topping
    1½ cups chopped zucchini
    1 cup chopped broccoli
    ½ cup crumbled tofu (optional)
    2 - 3 tablespoons olive oil
    ½ teaspoon oregano
    ¼ teaspoon rock salt
    1 cup pesto
    1 cup paneer, ricotta or goat cheese
    1 handful pine nuts

Sauté the veggies and tofu in olive oil and spices until the color of the veggies becomes brighter. Spread pesto, veggies, pine nuts and cheese onto crust in that order and bake for 10–15 minutes at 375F.

Summer Soup (serves 2)
Preparation time: 10 minutes
    1 large peeled, seeded cucumber, chopped to bite-sized pieces
    2 cups chopped spinach or other greens
    3 tablespoons sunflower oil
    ½ teaspoon grated ginger
    ½ teaspoon mustard seeds
    ½ teaspoon fennel seeds
    ¼ teaspoon rock salt
    1 handful fresh, chopped cilantro or parsley

Warm the oil in a pot and add the ginger, salt, mustard seeds and fennel seeds. Simmer until the aroma comes up and the mustard seeds pop, then add the greens and enough water to cover the bottom of the pot. Cover and simmer for 3-5 minutes. Then add the cucumber, stir and enough water to cover the veggies. Cover and simmer for 3-5 minutes or until slightly soft. Serve warm or at room temperature. Garnish with fresh cilantro or parsley.

Tahini Dressing (serves 4-6)
Preparation time: 5 minutes
    ½ cup olive or sunflower oil
    3 tablespoons tahini
    Juice of ½ fresh lime
    1 tablespoon raw honey
    1 teaspoon cumin powder
    1 teaspoon coriander powder
    ½ teaspoon ginger powder
    ½ teaspoon salt
    ¼ teaspoon black pepper
    1 medium avocado, peel and pit removed
    ½ cup water

Warm the oil in a pan and add cumin, coriander, ginger, salt and pepper. Simmer until the aroma comes up. Mix all ingredients together and blend. Store the mixture in the refrigerator in a glass jar. Stir before using and serve on whole grains or steamed vegetables.

Another option is to grind in one handful of peeled almonds or macadamia nuts. Use your creativity and play with moderate amounts of each.

Mixed Vegetables (serves 4)
Preparation time: 20 minutes

    2 cups augmenting vegetable, such as carrots, zucchini, winter squash or sweet potato
    1½ cup extractive vegetable, such as broccoli, cauliflower or kale
    2 tablespoons ghee
    ¾ teaspoon black mustard seeds
    ½ teaspoon sesame seeds
    Pinch of asafoetida
    ½ teaspoon coriander powder
    ¼ teaspoon cinnamon
    ½ teaspoon fresh grated ginger
    ¼ teaspoon turmeric powder
    ½ teaspoon rock salt
    ½–1 cup water

Wash, trim and cut vegetables into bite-sized pieces. Warm the ghee in a saucepan or deep sauté pan. Add the fresh ginger, mustard seeds, sesame seeds and asafoetida. Stir gently until seeds pop. Then add coriander, cinnamon, turmeric and salt and simmer until the aroma comes up. Stir in vegetables and coat with spices. Reduce heat, cover and cook for 5 minutes. Stir and add water as desired. Cook until vegetables are tender, 7–15 minutes, depending on the chosen vegetables and your pan.

Masala (enough for a few meals)
Preparation time: less than 10 minutes
    1 teaspoon ground cloves
    1 teaspoon ground cardamom
    1 teaspoon black peppercorns
    5 bay leaves
    1 teaspoon cinnamon
    2 teaspoon cumin seeds
    4 teaspoon coriander seeds

Grind the spices together with a mortar and pestle or blender until fine. This is a warming recipe, so use small amounts to stimulate digestion in cold winter weather. Use in vegetable recipes or soups. Be creative and see what works. Store masala in a glass or metal container in a dark cabinet.

Tamarind Chutney (serves many)
Preparation time: 5–10 minutes
> 3 teaspoons tamarind paste (use fresh tamarind if available)
> 1 tablespoon shredded dry coconut
> ½ teaspoon lime juice
> ½ teaspoon coriander powder
> ½ teaspoon cumin powder
> ¼ teaspoon turmeric powder
> ¼ teaspoon ginger powder
> Pinch of rock salt
> 3 tablespoons sesame oil

Sauté ingredients in warm sesame oil. Serve at room temperature.

Turmeric and Cumin Chutney (serves many)
Preparation time: 10 minutes
 1 teaspoon split mung beans
 ½ cup fresh turmeric
 ¼ cup cumin seeds
 5 tablespoons grated fresh ginger
 1 cup water
 ½ cup cilantro
 ½ cup lime juice
 ½ teaspoon rock salt
 Pinch of ground black pepper

In a blender, grind the split mung beans to powder. Chop or grate the turmeric into small pieces or a paste and add to blender along with cumin, ginger, and water. Blend to a paste and add the cilantro, lime, salt, and pepper. Good for balancing hot food.

Mint Chutney (serves many)
Preparation time: less than 10 minutes
    1 bunch fresh cilantro
    1 bunch fresh mint leaves
    2 tablespoons lime juice
    ¼ teaspoon ground rock salt
    ⅛ teaspoon cayenne pepper
    4 tablespoons fresh plain yogurt or buttermilk

Blend all ingredients together until smooth. Store in a glass jar in the refrigerator and use within three days.

Date and Ginger Chutney (serves many)
Preparation time: 5–10 minutes
    1 cup dates (fresh if available, or soak dried dates for one hour)
    2 tablespoons fresh ginger
    ½ teaspoon rock salt
    2 teaspoons fresh lime juice
    4 tablespoons water

Chop and pit dates. Grate ginger. Combine all ingredients in blender until smooth. This chutney is sweet and cooling, promoting strength and vitality.

Fig Tart (serves 6–8)
Preparation time: 1½ hours, mostly unattended
   Crust
   2 cups of flour (1 cup barley flour and 1 cup whole wheat flour)
   ½ teaspoon natural mineral salt or ground rock salt
   ⅛ teaspoon cinnamon (optional)
   ½ cup coconut oil (alternatives are ghee or almond oil)
   6–8 tablespoons cold water
   Chopped raw pecans or macadamia nuts

Preheat oven to 375F. Mix all dry ingredients with your clean hands. Add coconut oil to the dry mixture and mix until thoroughly absorbed. Stir in just enough water to hold the dough together in a ball. Cover the bowl and chill in the refrigerator for 30 minutes.

Press dough into a glass or stainless steel pan using your fingers. Sprinkle chopped raw pecans or macadamia nuts over the crust and bake for 5 minutes at 375F.

Filling
   1–2 pounds fresh ripe figs

Puree clean figs in a blender. If fresh figs are not available, reconstitute dried figs by soaking in water for 4 to 6 hours until they are very soft. Blend the figs with the soaking water.

Spread fig puree into tart crust. Bake for 20 minutes at 375F. Enjoy warm or at room temperature!

Muffins (makes about 20 muffins)
preparation time: 25 minutes
    2 cups flour (whole wheat with barley or oat flour)
    1 cup brown rice flour
    ½ cup flax meal
    ½ teaspoon nutmeg
    ½ teaspoon cinnamon
    ½ teaspoon cardamom
    ¾ teaspoon natural mineral salt
    ⅓ cup almond or sunflower oil
    3 handfuls of peeled/chopped almonds (optional)
    ½ cup maple syrup or natural unrefined sugar
    1-2 cups water

Preheat oven to 375F. Mix all dry ingredients together with nuts. Add oil and water until the flour is wet and thoroughly mixed into a soft, sticky dough.

Handle the dough as little as possible as you shape the muffins on a stainless sheet or glass dish. The shape may be irregular; this is okay. Bake at 375F for about 15 minutes until a toothpick comes out clean. The cooking time will vary depending on the size of your muffins, thickness of the pan and your oven. You can also make a savory variety with fresh ginger and fennel powder.

Ginger Pecan Muffins (makes about 10 muffins)
Preparation time: 25 minutes
    2 cups whole wheat or spelt flour
    2 cups barley flour
    1 teaspoon natural mineral salt
    1 tablespoon freshly grated ginger
    ¾ cup chopped pecans
    ⅓ cup ghee

Preheat oven to 375F. Combine dry ingredients thoroughly. Then add ginger, ghee and nuts, with enough water to make a sticky dough, mixing thoroughly.

Using your hands, shape the muffins on a stainless cookie sheet or glass baking dish. Bake at 375F for 15 minutes until a toothpick comes out clean. The time will vary a bit depending on the size of your muffins and your oven.

Pumpkin and Sweet Potato Pie (serves 4)
Preparation time: 1 hour, mostly unattended
    2 cups steamed or baked pumpkin squash
    2 cups steamed or baked sweet potato
    2–3 tablespoons ghee
    ½ teaspoon cinnamon
    10 threads saffron
    1 cup cow milk or rice milk (if steamed sweet potato or squash, use the liquid from steaming)
    ½ cup finely chopped pecans (optional)

Preheat oven to 375F. Place cooked pumpkin squash and sweet potato in blender with ghee and enough milk to blend easily. Stir in spices. Prepare a simple crust as in the Fig Tart recipe above. After lightly baking the crust, transfer the blended mixture to the baking dish. Sprinkle the pecans on top. Bake for 15-20 minutes. Let cool and serve. You can use carrots in place of the squash or sweet potato. If you are using a pressure cooker, use a small amount of water or milk to cook the sweet potato and pumpkin squash. This recipe is tasty without the crust.

Yogurt Lassi (serves 2)
Preparation time: 5 minutes or less
    ½ cup freshly made plain yogurt
    ½ cup water
    ⅛ teaspoon cumin powder
    ⅛ teaspoon coriander powder
    ⅛ teaspoon fennel powder
    ⅛ teaspoon ground black pepper
    Pinch of rock salt

Blend all ingredients for about one minute or put in a jar and shake vigorously. This drink aids digestion. Serve it at room temperature at the end of your meal, about one half per person. This is a savory lassi.

You may also like a sweet lassi by changing the spices above to ⅛ teaspoon cardamom, a pinch of cinnamon, and ½ teaspoon maple syrup. Adjust the spices using the spice guide in "The Basics of Preparing Food" to balance your doshas.

Raisin Drink (serves 1)
¼ cup raisins
1 cup water
⅛ teaspoon cardamom
⅛ teaspoon cinnamon

Soak raisins in water over night or for at least 4 hours. Consume the liquid. This drink is helpful for people with anemia, constipation and for increasing energy.

KITCHADI RECIPES FOR CLEANSING AND ENJOYMENT

Kitchadi is a simple soupy combination of rice and split mung beans with herbs and spices. Whole mung beans may be used instead but they must be soaked for 6-8 hours in advance of cooking. There are variations of ingredients to focus on balancing dosha, supporting agni, cleansing specific organs, healing and balancing. Kitchadi is easily digested and assimilated so that agni has an opportunity to rebuild and balance. It is excellent to eat if your immune system is feeling compromised or agni feels weak. Have it all day one day of the week for great results.

Simple Kitchadi (serves 4)
Preparation time: 1 hour, mostly unattended
 ½ cup basmati rice
 ¼ cup split mung beans
 3 tablespoons ghee
 1 teaspoon cumin seeds
 1 teaspoon coriander seeds
 ⅛ teaspoon asafoetida
 1 strip kombu cut into small pieces
 4 to 6 cups water (or more to reach desired consistency)
 ½ teaspoon rock salt
 1 tablespoon fresh grated ginger root
 1 teaspoon turmeric, fresh or powder
 ½ teaspoon cardamom
 2–4 cups freshly chopped vegetables such as carrots and greens

Wash the rice and split mung beans until the water runs clear. Warm the ghee in a pan and simmer the cumin seeds, coriander seeds, and asafoetida until the aroma comes up. Then add the rest of the spices and stir. Add the rice, split mung beans, and kombu, stir together, and simmer for 1–2 minutes more. Add 4 cups of water and simmer for 45 minutes with the lid on the pot. You may want to add more water to reach your desired consistency.

For a **cooling kitchadi**, use 6–10 inches of burdock root, 1 cup green beans, 1 teaspoon fennel seeds, and leave out the ginger and mung beans. Good for clearing the kidneys, purifying the blood, and reducing pitta.

For a **warming kitchadi**, increase the cardamom to ¾ teaspoon, add ½ teaspoon black peppercorns, 1 large bay leaf, ¾ teaspoon cinnamon, and ¼ teaspoon clove. After cooking all of the spices in ghee, place in a blender and grind thoroughly. Add this blended paste to the kitchadi. This kitchadi is good for stimulating digestion and circulation. It is balancing for vata and increasing for pitta. Reduce the ghee for kapha imbalance.

For a **digestive kitchadi**, add 3 bay leaves and add 1 teaspoon of dry oregano. This kitchadi is good for stimulating digestion without aggravating pitta.

For **cleansing the liver and gall bladder**, substitute sunflower oil for the ghee and ½ cup pearl barley for the rice. Add ½ teaspoon black mustard seeds to the spice preparation. When adding water also add 6–8 inches chopped burdock root and 1 tablespoon chopped, dry dandelion root. About 15–20 minutes before cooking time is complete, add broccoli and or dark leafy greens such as collards or kale for the vegetables. This kitchadi is diuretic and mildly laxative.

For **cleansing the kidneys**, substitute ½ cup adzuki beans for the split mung beans. Soak beans 6–8 hours in advance or cook in pressure cooker until soft. Increase the asafoetida to ½ teaspoon, and add ¼ teaspoon fennel seeds, 2 bay leaves, 3 curry leaves, ⅛ teaspoon cinnamon, and ¾ teaspoon ground rock salt. Leave out the ginger. For the vegetables, add 8–10 inches burdock root and one large acorn squash chopped into small pieces. This kitchadi is diuretic and cleansing for the kidneys. It is balancing for vata and kapha. Add chopped fresh cilantro to pacify pitta.

Sweet Potato Kitchadi (serves 4)
Preparation time: 1 hour, mostly unattended
 ½ cup basmati rice
 ¼ cup split mung beans
 1 inch grated fresh ginger
 2 tablespoons shredded coconut (fresh or dried)
 1 teaspoon turmeric
 ½ cup cilantro leaves
 3 tablespoons ghee
 8 green cardamom pods
 8 whole cloves
 11 black peppercorns
 3-inch piece cinnamon stick (optional)
 3 bay leaves
 1 large sweet potato, cubed

Rinse the split mung beans and brown rice. Blend ginger, coconut, turmeric, and cilantro with enough water to blend easily. In a large pot, melt ghee over medium heat and sauté cardamom pods, cloves, peppercorns, cinnamon stick, and bay leaves for 3-5 minutes. Then add the ginger blend and sauté for a few more minutes until lightly cooked. Next, add the split mung beans and rice and simmer a few more minutes. Add 4 cups of water (or more to reach your desired consistency). Turn heat to simmer and cook for 25 minutes. Add the sweet potatoes and more water as needed then cook for another 20 minutes. This kitchadi is good for stimulating digestion and reducing excess vata and kapha. Not recommended if you have excess pitta.

RECIPE FOR PEACE, FREEDOM, AND JOY
Slow down; look where you are heading.

Surrender self-will; be in the unknown and let life unfold.

Give your lower intellect a break; be quiet and listen to your innermost self in the higher intellect.

Attend to your choices and results; liberate yourself with self-responsibility.

Cultivate consciousness; learn to be in life.

Appendix B _ Wellness Journal

Use this journal as a tool to learn to relate what you eat and consume to how you are feeling. Copy this page and complete the information throughout the day for three weeks. It will help you become more aware of your patterns and the effect on you. This is an easy way to identify the source of problems.

Wellness Journal				
Date	Time	Time	Time	Time
Food				
Beverages				
Herbs and Supplements				
Sadhana (spiritual practices) Yoga Pranayama Meditation/mantra Asana Other				
Self-Care Gum and teeth Walk Mantra Other				

Sleep Schedule Wake up time Go to bed time Hours of sleep				
Physical Overall comfort Temperature Gut condition (gas, agni) Bowel movements, number and quality Skin condition Breath/tongue				
Mental Overall comfort Clarity Other				
Emotional Overall comfort Mood Temperament				
How do you feel?				

Appendix C - Chart of the Six Tastes

The chart below will assist you to balance the tastes in your meals. The pungent, bitter, and astringent tastes are cleansing in nature. The sweet, sour, and salty tastes are nourishing. In excess, anything can cause imbalance. Moderation is the key.

Elements	Taste	Qualities	Balances	Excess provokes	Vipak
Earth, water	Sweet	oily, heavy, cool	vata, pitta	kapha	sweet
Earth, fire	Sour	oily, heavy, warm	vata	pitta, kapha	sour
Water, fire	Salty	oily, heavy, warm	vata	pitta, kapha	sweet
Fire, air	Pungent	dry, light, hot	vata, kapha	pitta, vata	pungent
Air, ether	Bitter	dry, light, cold	kapha, pitta	vata	pungent
Air, earth	Astringent	dry, light, cool	kapha, pitta	vata	pungent

Appendix D - Chart of Elements and Corresponding Foods

The following chart will help you relate your foods to the elements.

Elements	Foods
Earth	augmenting vegetables, most nuts and seeds, some grains including wheat and rice, fresh coconut meat, sea vegetables (minerals), beans, meat, mushrooms
Water	dairy, juicy fruits (e.g., papaya, melons, grapes, oranges), juicy vegetables (e.g., cucumber and zucchini), coconut water
Fire	hot peppers, black pepper, cinnamon, cloves, ginger, asafoetida, garlic, onions, sour fruits (e.g., pineapple, lemons, grapefruit, tamarind, cranberries), alcohol, tobacco
Air	dried fruits, raw vegetables, extractive vegetables (e.g., broccoli, cabbages, sprouts, cauliflower), most beans
Ether	sprouts, fresh vegetable juice, algae, caffeine, drugs (e.g., alcohol, marijuana, cocaine, tobacco, anesthetics)

Appendix E _ Chart of Cooking Techniques

The following chart outlines cooking techniques and the qualities they impart to food.

	Qualities	Information
Baking	soft, heavy, dense, sweet	Baking is slow, resulting in the sweetest taste from food, least change of shape.
Blending	smooth, soft, thick, fine	Chunky food becomes creamy and smooth. Creamy soups, gravies, curries. Grain, beans, root vegetables, nuts, and seeds become creamy butters.
Boiling	lightest, soft, mobile	Takes the nutrients out of the ingredients and into the liquid. Suggested for very weak agni.
Sauté/par boiling	oily, moist, heavy	Keeps some of the nutrients, liquid, and flavor within the food.
Soaking	soft, moist	Softening dried beans, rehydrating dried fruits.
Sprouting	light, rough, dry, clear	Sprouted seeds, beans, and nuts are much lighter.
Steaming	light, soft, mobile	Good for light cooking of delicate foods.
Toasting	dry, hard, light, bitter	Good for lightening seeds, nuts, and grains.

Glossary

agni – digestive fire; transformative energy.

ama – metabolic toxins resulting from undigested foods or emotions.

Ayurveda - the science of life or living.

centenarians – people who live past one hundred years.

chakra – originates from ancient Yoga systems and the Sanskrit language literally meaning wheel or disk; spinning vortex of energy in and around the body; centers of activity for processing prana, life force.

clearing out – letting go of the past emotions and feelings that are being carried around.

codependent behavior – destructive patterns of living including attempting to control others, denial, low self-esteem, and over-compliance.

consciousness – awareness of one's existence, sensations, thoughts, surroundings, and impact.

dhal – or split mung dhal, whole mung beans with the hull removed and split.

digestive – an herb that stimulates digestion.

doshas – the three primary organizing principles of the body that determine the individual constitution; they are vata, pitta, and kapha; when in balance they bring harmony and when out of balance they stimulate disease.

"eating over" – emotional eating related to avoiding some particular feeling or emotion.

ego – self-centered consciousness; edging god out; the seeming separation between humans and their source within.

ghee – butter that has been cooked to a slightly extractive state rather than congestive as butter is.

gunas – attributes or aspects of nature consisting of sattva, rajas, and tamas. also called mahagunas.

kapha – earth and water constitution, dosha.

karma – the law of cause and effect, what you sow is what you reap; a circle of completion.

inner child – the aspect of the psyche that remains as the child.

innermost truth – knowingness from conscious connection to Divine source.

innermost self – the source within realized through direct consciousness; higher intellect.

peristalsis – the natural flexing movement of the colon.

pitta – fire and water constitution, dosha.

prana – the flow of intelligence, or life force; also the breath.

processing – consciously walking through feelings, allowing them to come and pass freely; letting go.

rajas – the quality of movement, activity, energy.

sacred – connection to the Divine source.

samskara – impressions, the process of conditioning.

sattva – the quality of evenness, compassion, balance and harmony, the light.

tamas – the quality of dullness, lethargy, inertia, the darkness.

vata – air and ether constitution, dosha.

vegan – one who does not eat any animal products.

vegetarian – one who eats no animal flesh but may eat honey and dairy.

vipak – post-digestive effect of food.

virya – heating and cooling effect of food or drink.

Endnotes

1. U.S. National Center for Health Statistics, *Health*, United States, 2007.

2. Sky Bamhart, "Where's the real food,"*The Maui Weekly*, June 08, 2006.

3. If you are interested in learning more about water and the possibilities, read *The Hidden Messages in Water* by Masaru Emoto, translated by David A. Thayne (Hillsboro, Oregon: Beyond Words Publishing, 2004).

Bibliography

Christensen, Alice. *Yoga of the Heart*. American Yoga Association and the Philip Lief Group, Inc., 1998. Highly recommended for further understanding of Yoga and modern living.

Easwaran, Eknath. *The Bhagavad Gita for Daily Living*. 3 vols. Nilgiri Press, 1975. Excellent for perspective and applying the principles of Yoga to Western living.

Frawley, Dr. David. *Ayurvedic Healing: A Comprehensive Guide*. Salt Lake City: Passage Press, 1989. In-depth reference for Ayurveda.

Gibran, Kahlil. *The Prophet*. New York: Alfred A. Knopf, Inc., 1923.

Grabhorn, Lynn. *Beyond the Twelve Steps*. Charlottesville, Virginia: Hampton Roads Publishing Co., 1992.

Kozak, Sandra Summerfield. *Forgiveness: The Path to Happiness*. Honesdale, Pennsylvania: Himilayan Institute Press, 2005. Light Transitions Tapes, 293 Andrew Ct. Benicia, CA 94510, www.internationalyogastudies.com. Highly recommended for daily living.

Lad, Vasant. *Textbook of Ayurveda Fundamental Principles*. Albuquerque: The Ayurvedic Press, 2002. In-depth reference for Ayurveda.

Merton, Thomas. *The Living Bread.* New York: Farrar, Straus & Cudahy, 1956.

Morningstar, Amadea. *The Ayurvedic Cookbook for Westerners.* Twin Lakes, Wisconsin: Lotus Press, 1995. Highly recommended for Western recipes from the Ayurvedic perspective.

Morningstar, Amadea, and Urmila Desai. *The Ayurvedic Cookbook.* Wilmot, Wisconsin: Lotus Light, 1990. Highly recommended.

Pole, Sebastian. *Ayurvedic Medicine: The Principles of Traditional Practice.* Philadelphia: Churchill Livingstone Elsevier, 2006. In-depth reference for Ayurveda.

Ruskin, John. *Emotional Clearing.* New York: Wyler & Co., 1993. Good for integrating Eastern and Western approaches to spiritual connectedness.

Shiva, Vandana. *Manifestos on the Future of Food & Seed.* Cambridge: South End Press, 2007. Excellent information on the state of our food and seed supplies.

Svoboda, Dr. Robert E. *Prakruti: Your Ayurvedic Constitution.* Albuquerque: Geocom, 1988. Highly recommended for further understanding of Ayurveda.

Tiwari, Maya. *Ayurveda: A Life of Balance.* Rochester: Lotus Press, Healing Arts Press, 1995. Highly recommended for deeper understanding of Ayurvedic healing modalities.

About the Author

MYRA E. LEWIN, BA, MBA, AP

Myra Lewin has studied and practiced Ayurveda and Yoga for nearly 30 years. She has guided thousands of people to reclaim their natural, balanced state of health and overcome issues, including addiction, eating disorders, and autoimmune disorders. As founder and director of Hale Pule Ayurveda & Yoga (halepule.com), based on Kaua'i, Myra offers a range of opportunities to learn about and heal with these transformational sciences, including professional training in Yoga and Ayurveda, as well as health consultations.

Made in the USA
San Bernardino,
CA